FEATURES

KNITTING

CROCHET

COOKERY

Cover by Susan Mayer.
Sequin top from Frank Usher, earrings by Adrien Mann.

Printed and published in Great Britain by D. C. Thomson & Co., Ltd., 185 Fleet Street, London EC4A 2HS

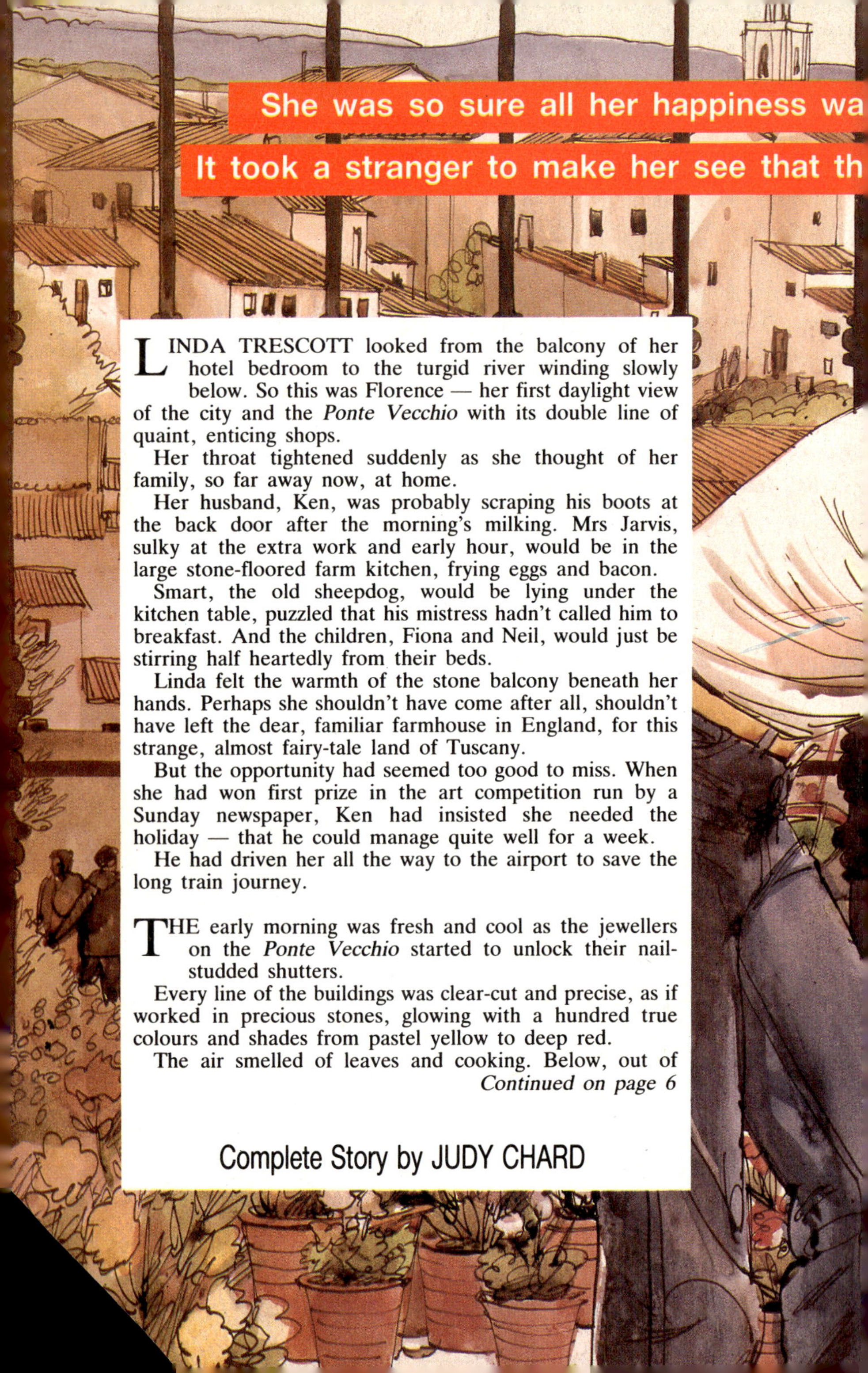

She was so sure all her happiness wa

It took a stranger to make her see that th

LINDA TRESCOTT looked from the balcony of her hotel bedroom to the turgid river winding slowly below. So this was Florence — her first daylight view of the city and the *Ponte Vecchio* with its double line of quaint, enticing shops.

Her throat tightened suddenly as she thought of her family, so far away now, at home.

Her husband, Ken, was probably scraping his boots at the back door after the morning's milking. Mrs Jarvis, sulky at the extra work and early hour, would be in the large stone-floored farm kitchen, frying eggs and bacon.

Smart, the old sheepdog, would be lying under the kitchen table, puzzled that his mistress hadn't called him to breakfast. And the children, Fiona and Neil, would just be stirring half heartedly from their beds.

Linda felt the warmth of the stone balcony beneath her hands. Perhaps she shouldn't have come after all, shouldn't have left the dear, familiar farmhouse in England, for this strange, almost fairy-tale land of Tuscany.

But the opportunity had seemed too good to miss. When she had won first prize in the art competition run by a Sunday newspaper, Ken had insisted she needed the holiday — that he could manage quite well for a week.

He had driven her all the way to the airport to save the long train journey.

THE early morning was fresh and cool as the jewellers on the *Ponte Vecchio* started to unlock their nail-studded shutters.

Every line of the buildings was clear-cut and precise, as if worked in precious stones, glowing with a hundred true colours and shades from pastel yellow to deep red.

The air smelled of leaves and cooking. Below, out of

Continued on page 6

Complete Story by JUDY CHARD

n the past.
uture could hold

...THE PRECIOUS YEARS

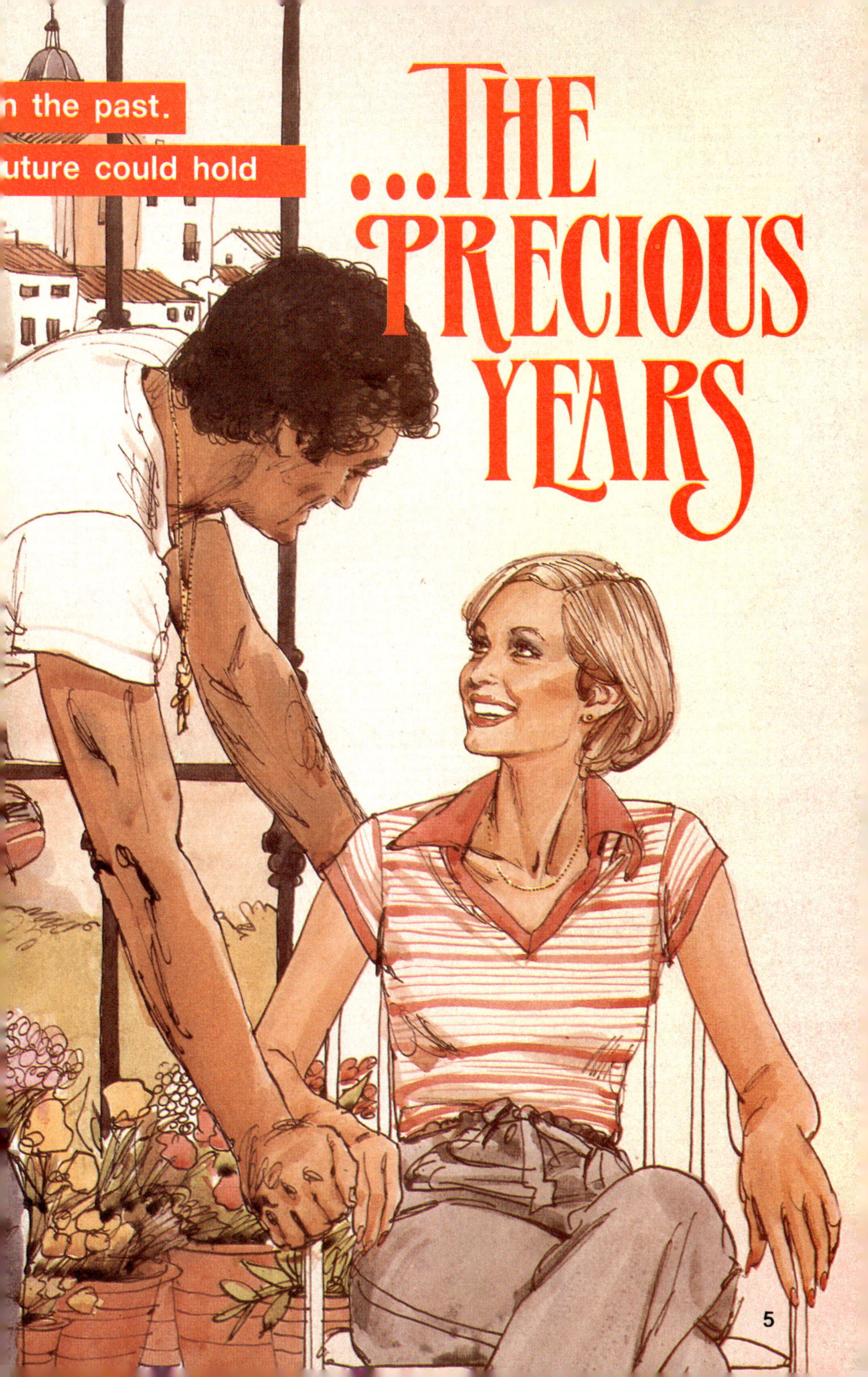

sight, was the faint clatter of china and the lilt of Italian voices. Soon she would be trying hard to capture all this on canvas.

Linda hadn't painted for years, but the competition had rekindled her imagination. The judges had liked her treatment of the bluebell wood — the sunshine through the leaves, the detailed clumps of flowers in the foreground, giving life and authenticity to the whole work.

She had studied at a local college when she left school, and was in her second year when she had come to Devon on a sketching holiday with two other girls. Then, too, they had found the bluebell wood which had just asked to be painted.

Setting up their stools and easels, they had been too absorbed to see the cows which had gathered in a silent, curious ring around them.

Suddenly Linda had looked up and given a little shriek.

They were completely surrounded by the animals, who gazed at them with liquid eyes, their tails swishing gently, their breath sweet with spring grass.

That was how Linda had first met Ken. The three girls had sat petrified, not daring to move. They were all townbred and had no idea what to do. Then, to their relief, a young man had come swinging down the lane, a sheepdog at his heels.

When he saw the expressions of horror on the girls' faces, he had burst out laughing, and sent his dog to round up the cows and return them to the lane. When they had shambled off, he came back to tell them it was safe to move.

"They wouldn't hurt you," he'd said, the laughter still in his voice. "They're curious, that's all, like most ladies!"

He invited them to tea at the farmhouse, where his ageing mother deftly set the long kitchen table with country fare — home-made bread, great bowls of yellow cream, and strawberry jam.

Ken had singled Linda out after tea, taking her round the barn and outhouses, showing her the cows safely chained in their stalls, chewing the roots and hay in gentle rhythm as the milk swished into the shining pails.

She had fallen in love with the old cob-walled farm, the folds of green hills — and with Ken as only a seventeen-year-old can.

And twelve months later they had married.

There had been a lot to learn. She'd had to conquer her nervousness of the animals — even Smart had frightened her when he jumped up in friendly greeting. And the hens had pecked her hands when she lifted them off their nests to collect the eggs.

Her first pregnancy had been difficult. She'd been sick and lethargic. The country-bred women seemed to take all this in their stride. To them, having babies was just another part of the cycle of farm life.

But after Neil's birth, everything had undergone a subtle change.

Then Fiona was born, and Linda gradually became part of the

farm, part of the countryside and Ken's family.

One by one, Ken's sisters had married and gone away to their husbands' farms, and Linda had settled down to that easy recurring rhythm that only the countrywomen know, with the everlasting and inevitable change of the seasons.

But with the children nearly grown up, she had found herself with more time on her hands.

It had been Ken's suggestion to get out the brushes and paints of her student days.

"Have another go at the bluebell wood," he'd said, grinning. "I've always had a soft spot for it."

And so she had begun to paint again. When the competition had been announced, Ken had told her to send in "Bluebell Wood."

"It'll win hands down," he'd said. And, of course, he'd been right.

Not that he was in any way artistic himself. He was a simple, basic man, deeply involved with his farm, while she had always loved books and art.

Winning this prize had filled her with the old remembered delight in her talent, and brought the realisation of a half-forgotten dream — a visit to Florence, art centre of the world.

AFTER breakfast on her first morning in Florence, she decided to ignore the museums and galleries for the time being.

Instead, she wandered the streets looking for all the places she had read about: the Straw Market, hidden beneath hats and baskets, the *Ponte Vecchio,* where children perched like merry starlings, tanned a golden brown in their T-shirts and jeans.

When she reached the *Piazzale Michelangelo,* high up at the back of the city, the enchanting view of the valley of the Arno lay at her feet.

There was a small restaurant with a bright awning, and she suddenly realised she was hungry. She pushed aside the bead curtain and was welcomed by a smiling proprietor.

The meal was excellent, *bollito misti* with a green salad, the various meats forked from a huge cauldron, which was wheeled to her table, on to a carving platter.

The waiter brought a glass of ruby chianti — a local wine, highly praised. She sipped it while he waited.

"Bene grazie," she said shyly, studying the wine, smooth and warm as tawny autumn sunshine.

At that moment there was the sound of approaching cars, and what was obviously a wedding party swept into the café, overflowing to the tables set outside under the trees.

The men were in their best Sunday suits and the girls wore fantastic hats. They all sat chattering and smiling gaily.

To Linda the bride and 'groom looked ridiculously young . . . She smiled at their undisguised joy and felt a sudden stab of loneliness.

They were followed in by an older man, also a member of the party, with silvered dark hair and rugged, almost handsome features.

He carried a guitar under his arm and was immediately

OUR AFRICAN QUEEN

IF anybody had a pet with personality we had.

Having lived in Northern Rhodesia, now Zambia, of course, for fifteen years my husband and I toured the whole of the Northern Territory. As civil servants, we were moved to a new post every two or three years, and resided in Livingstone, Lusaka, Kitwe, Abercorn and finally Mongu in Barotseland.

It was whilst we were stationed in Mongu, which was mainly bush country, that Sheba came into our lives.

One day an African came to the door carrying a crudely-made wicker cage. Inside were two of the funniest little creatures you ever did see. They looked like a couple of glove puppets.

"Cheetahs, Bwana," the African said. "Five shillings each . . . ?"

My husband, being a lover of all animals, bought them right away. But the poor things were so weak we hardly knew where to start caring for them.

I began with a fountain-pen filler, squeezing drops of milk into the cheetahs every two hours. Sadly, one of them died within twenty-four hours, but the other, which we called Sheba, hung on and gradually became stronger.

Soon the filler was replaced by a baby's feeding bottle. After a couple of weeks on this — and by then Sheba had bitten through three teats — we thought it time to try her with something more solid.

A saucer of raw minced meat went down very well, and from then on she began to thrive.

I must say at this stage Sheba was a little spitfire. But we also had Stanley, a dachshund puppy, and,

encouraged, with cheers and clapping, to provide the entertainment.

Linda dreaded the inevitable Italian pop song which would take the magic from the scene, but she was surprised when he began to sing an old Italian ballad in a rich, deep baritone.

She sat entranced, and was startled to realise his blue gaze had come to rest on her where she sat, half in shadow.

Then, still gazing at her, he began to pluck out a different melody

BY ROSE E. MATTHEWS

thankfully they used to play together. At that time they were almost the same size.

As Sheba got bigger she used to travel round with us in the Land-Rover, sitting between my husband and myself on the front seat. In fact, in those early days she usually climbed up on my knees and wouldn't budge for anything.

As she got bigger, though, we had to put a stop to this as she was blocking up the windscreen...

At home, Sheba just liked to relax. Although we fixed up a pen in the back garden, invariably she spent her time in the lounge with us. She would take over the settee completely, and heaven help anyone who wanted to sit alongside her — a little nip and a shove and you were off!

She did allow me to give her a good rub down, and let me clean her eyes and ears without protest.

Fortunately, too, we were able to get plenty of offal and raw meat for her. She came along fine and gradually became a good-sized animal, roughly about the size of a fully-grown Alsatian.

SHEBA was the perfect bodyguard. When we went out shopping in the car, we could leave it unlocked with Sheba safely inside. No-one would come within a mile of her!

It was the same in the evenings. If we had occasion to go out, a vigilant Sheba was left in the lounge.

There, with her front paws on the window ledge, she would wait impatiently for our return. She knew the minute our car entered the drive and would come bounding to the front door. As you might guess, we never had a burglary.

It was so funny at meal times. Sheba and Stanley would sit at the fridge door side by side — the "long and the short," we called them, for by this time Stanley could walk under Sheba with ease.

The time eventually arrived, however, when we were due to return to the UK on retirement. We found Stanley a home without any trouble, but it was a problem to know what to do with Sheba.

Luckily, about this time, she was becoming quite well known. Her photograph appeared in the local paper with a small paragraph announcing that her owners were about to leave Africa.

We received dozens of letters from people who wished to adopt or buy her, and we even had a letter from the King's African Rifles, asking if they could have her for a mascot.

In the meantime, though, we had heard from some friends of ours — a married couple who had a hotel on the edge of a game reserve. They were very keen to have Sheba, and promised that, should she get to the stage when she wanted to be free, they would part with her at once. So it was decided...

With sad hearts we set off on our final trip with Sheba. On arrival at the hotel we found that our friends had prepared a wonderful place for her, with plenty of ground to roam in, and again she had her own little house to sleep in.

We stayed overnight. Then the next morning we drove slowly away. The last I saw of our dearly-loved pet were those big soulful eyes watching us leave.

I'll never forget Sheba — our African queen. ■

— "Greensleeves" — and Linda was further drawn into the romantic web he had created.

When he stopped, the wedding party applauded loudly, and he started a conventional Italian love song. Realising she had been sitting for a long time with empty plates around her, Linda called for her bill.

Before she fell asleep that night she lay thinking of Ken, feeling a surge of homesickness and longing, in the big empty bed, as she watched darkness fall through the slats of the shutters.

THE next morning she set out for the Boboli Gardens to paint. It was all she had imagined, with dark avenues of ilex and cypress, the cool sound of water dripping into marble basins and emerald lizards lying motionless on the hot stones.

She sat on the steps of the arena and started to sketch, soon becoming absorbed in her work.

"Buongiorno, Signora . . ."

She swung round and found herself gazing into the intense eyes of the man who had sung in the café.

"H-hello," she said, and felt her face flush.

"May I sit beside you?"

"Of course." She felt a little bubble of excitement rise inside her as he looked over her shoulder at the drawing.

"Very good! You have made Neptune come alive. You are an artist for a living?"

"No, just a-an amateur." She had been going to say "housewife," but something had stopped her.

"But it is good — you have talent." His voice was filled with admiration and appreciation.

"You have, too — I enjoyed your singing very much. That song — 'Greensleeves' — I hadn't heard it sung that way before."

He smiled. "You would not. The words are my own."

"But it was beautiful! Are you a musician, then?"

He shook his head, almost regretfully. "I teach at the University in Roma — that is for money. For pleasure I have music." He paused. "But tell me about yourself. Why have you come here?"

"There's nothing much to tell. I won a competition, and a holiday in Florence was the prize." She didn't somehow want to explain about her farm-life and family yet.

"Then you are alone?"

She nodded, and he smiled at her with open delight. "I am Renato Minelli. And you?"

"Linda — Linda Trescott . . ." Suddenly a strange panic gripped her and she started to pick up her paints. "I must be getting back to the hotel . . ."

"But you can't spend your time here alone," he said, more animated now, gesticulating in a very Italian way. "Let me show you the city as the visitor does not see it, and then perhaps we can eat together?"

Linda looked down, seemingly engrossed in packing her equipment. Should she accept such an invitation? But why not? She wouldn't be here for long, and what harm could an evening of pleasant company and conversation do?

She looked up at him again, smiling gratefully.

"Thank you, that would be lovely."

"I'll be outside your hotel at eight."

Back in her room, Linda took off her dress and slip. Her figure was still slender and supple. She had a shower, made up carefully, and brushed out her hair, an odd tingle running through her at the sheer novelty at what she was doing.

The heat of the day lingered still in the streets, but it was cool beside the river. Renato showed her the old *Cimetero degli Inglesi* behind its spiked railings, and the grave of Elizabeth Barrett Browning, now covered by briars and oleanders.

The sky was pink in the last half-hour of sunlight as they turned back to the Boboli Gardens.

Then he led her to a tower with a spiral staircase leading to a room with a small bar where a young man was serving superb sandwiches and cold drinks.

He ordered wine and a plate of toasted sandwiches with olives, which they took out to the balcony.

Below them lay Florence, a haphazard collection of red roofs, domes and towers.

As they talked, Linda found herself becoming more articulate than she had been for a long time. All her half-formed thoughts translated easily into words now. She could have gone on for ever as one subject followed another.

She began to realise how alike Renato and she were — they had read and enjoyed the same books, loved the same music and paintings.

Here, she realised with a sudden shock, was something she had never tried to share with Ken. Talking to Renato, she was in a different world.

And he encouraged her to talk — arguing gently, putting forward his viewpoints. She even managed to talk about her family without feeling disloyal.

"The children grow away from you so gradually, you hardly notice it. Then suddenly they're talking about things they think you know nothing about — the modern poets, politics, new art forms."

"Then you don't join in their discussions?" He looked at her almost accusingly.

"No — no, I don't. I feel that would push them even further away. But it shouldn't, should it?"

"No, it shouldn't, you could probably teach each other a lot. Their modern inventiveness with your experience.

"And your husband?" he continued. "Do you share your thoughts with him?"

She looked down at her hands. "Of course I do, but —" She hesitated. "He has so much to do, running the farm. He has little time for the kind of things we've talked about."

"You could be surprised. Now your children have grown up, you must both have more time — time to be together. Think of the years ahead of you. These are the precious years."

He smiled suddenly and, calling the waiter, ordered more drinks. "I forgot — you are here to enjoy yourself, not to be preached at."

At last they fell silent. But their silence was one of unassailable

Continued on page 14

This soft, lacy sweater with a flattering ribbed collar is sure to draw admiring looks. Instructions are given to fit sizes 28-42 inch bust.

Materials Required. — Of **Twilleys Featherspun** 7 (8, 9) x 50 gram balls; one pair each of 3¼ mm, 3¾ mm and 4 mm (Nos. 10, 9 and 8) knitting needles; 3 buttons.

For best results it is essential to use the recommended yarn. If you have difficulty in obtaining the yarn, write direct, enclosing a stamped, addressed envelope, to the following address for stockists: H. G. Twilley Ltd., Roman Mill, Stamford, Lincolnshire PE9 1BG.

Measurements. — To fit bust 71-76 (81-91, 97-107) cm, *28-30 (32-36, 38-42) inch*; length, 53 (58, 63) cm, *20¾ (22¾, 24¾) inches*; sleeve seam, 40 (43, 46) cm, *15¾ (17, 18) inches*.

Tension. — 21 stitches and 26 rows to 10 cm, *4 inches*, over pattern on 4 mm needles.

Abbreviations. — K — knit; P — purl; st.(s) — stitch(es); tog. — together; y.fwd. — yarn forward; t.b.l. — through back of loop; cm — centimetres.

N.B. Figure in brackets ( ) refer to the larger sizes; where only one figure is given, this refers to all sizes. Figures in square brackets [ ] are worked the number of times stated.

Back.

Using 3¼ mm needles cast on 87 (103, 121) sts. and work in K1, P1 rib for 5 cm, *2 inches*, ending with a wrong-side row and increase one st. in last row on 2nd size only — 87 (104, 121) sts.

Change to 4 mm needles and work in pattern:

1st row. — Knit.

2nd row. — Purl.

3rd row. — K1, *[K2 tog. t.b.l.] 3 times, [y.fwd., K1] 5 times, y.fwd., [K2 tog.] 3 times; repeat from * to last st., K1.

4th row. — Knit.

These 4 rows form the pattern; repeat them until work measures approximately 45 (48, 51) cm, *17¾ (19, 20) inches*, ending with a 4th pattern row.**

PRETTY SENSATIONAL

Work in garter-st. (every row knit) for 8 (10, 12) cm, *3¼ (4, 4¾) inches*, ending with a wrong-side row.

Shape Neck.

Next row. — Cast off 26 (32, 37) sts., K34 (39, 46), cast off remaining 26 (32, 37) sts. Leave centre sts. on a holder.

Front.

Work as given for Back to **

Divide For Front Opening.

Next row. — K42 (50, 59), turn and leave remaining 45 (54, 62) sts. on a spare needle.

Next row. — Cast on 3 (4, 3) sts. for button band, knit to end. Continue on these 45 (54, 62) sts. in garter-st., work 11 rows, ending with a right-side row.

***__Next row.__ — Cast off 2 sts., knit to end.

Shape Neck.

Next row. — K35 (42, 48), turn and slip remaining 8 (10, 12) sts. on to a holder. Decrease one st. at neck edge on every row until 26 (32, 37) sts. remain, then continue without shaping until work measures the same as Back to shoulders, ending with a wrong-side row. Cast off.***

Return to the sts. on spare needle; with right side facing rejoin yarn and knit 4 rows.

Next row (buttonhole row). — K1, K2 tog., y.fwd., knit to end. Work 2 more buttonholes on every following 4th row, then knit 1 row, thus ending with a wrong-side row.

Work as for first side from *** to ***

Sleeves (Both Alike).

Using 3¼ mm needles cast on 35 (35, 45) sts., and work in K1, P1 rib for 5 cm, *2 inches*, ending with a right-side row.

Next row. — K0 (0, 1), knit twice into each st. to last 0 (0, 2) sts., K0 (0, 2) — 70 (70, 87) sts.

Change to 4 mm needles and work in pattern as on Back until sleeve measures approximately 39 (42, 45) cm, *15¼ (16½, 17¾) inches*, ending with a 4th pattern row. Work 4 rows in garter-st. Cast off loosely.

Collar.

Join shoulder seams.

Using 3¾ mm needles and with right side facing, slip 8 (10, 12) sts. of Right Front on to needle, pick up and K30 (33, 36) sts. up right front neck, K35 (40, 47) back neck sts., increase one st. in centre on 2nd size only, pick up and K30 (33, 36) sts. down left front neck, then knit remaining 8 (10, 12) sts. — 111 (127, 143) sts.

Next row. — Work in K1, P1 rib, increase 40 (44, 48) sts. evenly across the row — 151 (171, 191) sts.

Continue in rib until collar measures 18 (20, 22) cm, *7 (7¾, 8¾) inches*. Cast off loosely in rib.

To Make Up.

Do not press. Sew in sleeves, placing centre of sleeves to shoulder seams. Join side and sleeve seams. Sew down cast-on edge of button band. Sew on buttons.

MARY, MARY, QUITE CONTRARY . . .

My husband is very proud of our garden. And he tends it meticulously.

So he was pleased the other week to see our little girl politely stopping a neighbour's toddler from walking on the garden.

But he wasn't too flattered when he heard her shout:

"Get off my daddy's mud!"

Continued from page 11

happiness and peace, a feeling Linda knew she would never experience again but which would remain with her till she died.

"I lost my wife five years ago." He broke into her thoughts gently. "We had been married for twenty years. I thought she was unique — until I met you . . ,"

Linda turned away quickly, looking over the city, refusing to meet the look in his eyes.

As if he could read her mind he changed the mood abruptly.

"Tomorrow, we'll go to Fiesole, and I'll bring a picnic."

Turning back to him with the assurance of mundane things, she said, "No, please let me. The hotel will arrange it."

"Then I will bring the wine — and it will be the best this city has to offer for you, my dear."

His eyes held hers and this time she didn't turn away.

WHEN he had left her at the door of the hotel, she went to her room and lay on the bed without undressing. Sounds from the street drifted up through the latched shutters — all was dusk and stillness, perfumed and torpid.

She shut her eyes, luxuriating in the memories of the day — the sounds, the sun shining on his hair and skin, and those penetrating eyes.

When she awoke, the air smelled fresh, the sky was the pale depthless blue that promised another hot day. Beneath her balcony, the city was a hazy, shimmering shadow.

She felt like a young girl on her first date, looking at her watch every minute. She saw the fruit barrow in the street and ran downstairs to buy peaches for their picnic.

The small, shabby Italian wrapped the fruit carefully and pushed a huge bunch of fragrant mimosa into her hand — "For the Signora, to match her hair."

Back at the hotel, the receptionist handed her an air-letter. It was from Ken. She took it up to her room, her hands trembling as she opened it. She felt as if he were looking over her shoulder as she read it.

He told her every little detail of his life without her. There were no flowery phrases, but, knowing Ken, she knew the depth of feeling that had prompted him to write it.

We all miss you terribly, my darling. The house just isn't home without you . . .

Suddenly tears pricked her eyelids. It must have taken a lot for Ken to say that — Ken, the inarticulate, the unimaginative.

What a deep, tranquil love theirs was, made up of so many things — experiences of joy and sorrow that only years of marriage bring — things that could never be shared with anyone else but Ken. No-one . . .

And yet, how different her life would have been with someone like Renato . . .

But she'd had a good life with Ken, a full life. And perhaps the best was yet to come. What had Renato said — the precious years?

Suddenly she just wanted to go home, at once, back to the dear, familiar countryside she knew so well. Florence had become unreal.

She'd get her ticket changed, take an early plane, send Ken a cable. Already she noticed the mimosa was dropping its yellow, powdery pollen in the heat of the room.

She thought of the roses that climbed over the wall of the yard, back at the farm — Albertine, old fashioned, but heavy with sweet perfume as its pale pink petals fluttered on the summer breeze.

She sat down and drew some writing paper towards her. For a moment she sat remembering — their long conversations, his eyes, the brief touch of his hand — imagining what might have been. Then she started to write . . .

Renato, I am so sorry but I'm returning to England today. I will always treasure the memory of our time together. Forgive me — I shall never forget you. Thank you for everything. Linda.

Hearing a sharp knock at the door, she hurried across the room to open it.

A small, bright-eyed bell-boy stood beaming at her from the doorway, holding out his silver tray. "A note for you, Signora."

Linda took the note and put a few coins on the tray. Then she walked back into the room, tearing open the envelope with nervous fingers.

The writing was clear and precise, a few simple words that said so much: *Enjoy those precious years. Renato.*

Picking up her own letter, she screwed the two into a tight ball. Then she walked out on to the balcony and threw it to the river below.

If she hurried and changed her ticket she could just catch that early plane. She'd be back in England almost before she knew it . . .

And if she phoned Ken, he would come to the airport to meet her and together they would go home . . .

*** THE END ***

The

Complete Story by CHARLES C. O'CONNELL

THE road straightened for a mile before the village to tunnel beneath a bower of elms. It is a picturesque entrance to Kilmel and never fails to delight me. In early summer broad lances of sunlight filter through the foliage above like gossamer curtains of gold.

As had become my custom in the last week, I slowed the car to savour the beauty of the shadowed road — and I remain eternally grateful that I did. At the gates of Howard House, some hundred yards before the road enters the village, I nearly ran a girl down.

She was about twenty or so and came running from the sunken gateway right out in front of me. I jammed on the brakes and screamed to a stop a matter of feet from her. She made no effort to save herself. It was as though she were petrified with shock or fear.

I was cold and trembling with shock as I jerked open the door and

Captive Heart

Was his love enough to set her free from the prison she had chosen for herself?

got out. I was also in a towering rage.

"What the devil are you trying to do? Kill yourself?"

She looked at me as if she didn't understand what I had said, or indeed, why I should have spoken as I had. Her face was ashen and a strand of her long fair hair lay against her cheek like a thin scar.

"I'm sorry." Her voice was a whisper.

My anger was replaced by anxiety as my doctor's thinking took over. I had little doubt that she was badly shocked. My concern must have been obvious because she smiled faintly and her eyes closed for a moment.

"I'm all right. It was foolish of me to run out like that —" She broke off suddenly to look up and down as if she had just remembered the reason why she had come out on the road. A wild anxiety was in her eyes. She brushed her fingers across her forehead.

"Are you looking for something?" I asked. "A dog perhaps?"

I felt her eyes on my face and again I got the impression that she hadn't understood me.

"No. Not a dog," she said quickly. "Did you see a woman on the road?"

"No," I said. "I saw no-one but you."

She glanced behind her and I followed her gaze. From the gates

B

the drive curved to the right and was lost behind the ragged shrubs that flanked it.

"Do you live here?" I asked.

She answered without turning. "Yes."

"Let me see you to the house. I'm afraid you've been shocked. I'm Dr Keith Lindsay. My practice is in the village."

She turned her head immediately and I noticed that fear had replaced the anxiety in her eyes.

"I'm all right, thank you. You don't have to trouble yourself."

"It's no trouble," I said. "I can't leave you like —"

"I'm perfectly all right," she said quickly. "Will you please go."

Over her shoulder I saw something move and was startled to see a tall woman at the gates. As if my eyes had mirrored this sudden apparition, the girl turned around.

MOTHER!" The single word conveyed a wealth of relief tinged with a certain impatience. In a moment the girl was in the woman's arms.

I watched them in silence, listening with a sense of wonder to the small soothing sounds the woman was making.

"I'm afraid I nearly knocked your daughter down," I said.

The girl's mother looked up and smiled. She was the most striking woman I had ever seen. Her hair, streaked with white, swept back from her face in Spanish fashion. It matched her regal air and I had no doubt that she was once very beautiful.

Indeed, she was still lovely — a mature loveliness only slightly marred by a scar on the right side of her forehead. It was not completely hidden by her hair.

"You mustn't blame yourself," she said gently. "Carmel will be all right now." She stroked her daughter's hair. "Won't you, dear?"

"Yes, Mother," the girl said slowly.

"Come along then. We'll go home."

"She might enjoy a cup of hot, very sweet tea," I suggested as they moved away, "and keep her warm."

The woman paused, her arm still around her daughter.

"Are you a doctor?" she said.

"Yes."

I thought I saw a look of fear in her eyes. "Where do you work?" she asked.

"In the village. I'm doing locum for my uncle. My name is Keith Lindsay."

Even as I spoke, I felt she already knew that my student days were not so far behind me.

"It is very nice meeting you, Dr Lindsay," she said gravely. "My name's Stuart. Mrs Eve Stuart."

I became aware that the girl was looking at me. There were tears on her cheeks.

"I'm sorry for causing you so much trouble," she said.

"There, there," her mother soothed, "don't worry about it. You haven't caused any trouble. The doctor understands."

She led her daughter away and the encounter was over.

My anxiety for the girl compelled me to watch them until the shrubs hid them from my view. I got into the car and reluctantly drove to the village.

Although I was busy in the surgery for the rest of the day, the incident of the afternoon remained in my mind. However, an opportunity to talk about it presented itself that evening when my uncle telephoned.

He was supposed to be on a well-earned holiday, but I suspect he was worried about the patients he had entrusted into my hands for three weeks.

He wanted to know how things were going and I gave him a detailed run-down on all the people I had seen. He knew them all and grunted approval from time to time as I told him what I had prescribed.

There was nothing serious among the lot of them. Kilmel was a very healthy parish. In the end I told him of my near accident and enquired if he knew the two people I had met.

I was disappointed to learn that he hadn't seen them, although he'd heard that they had moved into Howard House a month before. He suggested that I check on the girl's condition at an early opportunity.

I CREATED the opportunity the next day. I drove down the lane and turned in the open gates of Howard House.

Within a moment, the house itself came into view, a great Georgian mansion set on a ragged field that had once been a lawn. The heavy hand of neglect and decay was evident everywhere.

Grass grew in tufts through the scant gravel on the frontage. The house looked deserted and the doorbell did not seem to work.

I found the heavy door-knocker stiff. I waited a moment and was about to knock again when the door was opened by Carmel's mother. Her impassive expression softened slowly.

"You're the young doctor of yesterday."

"I was worried about your daughter, so I thought I'd look in."

She opened the door wider. "You needn't worry. Carmel is quite well, but, please, come in."

She led me through the hall to a spacious room. The sun pouring through the open french window threw a broad bar of light across the faded carpet. The furniture was scanty and Victorian. The corniced ceiling was peeling in places.

"We've just moved in," said the woman. "There is a lot to be done to make the house comfortable and most of my own furniture is in Scotland still. The only thing this place has at the moment is privacy.

"Nobody should bother us here. I hope Carmel will be happy here. I'll get her for you."

I was slightly embarrassed. "There's no necessity, really. As long as she's all right."

There was a certain appeal in her smile. “I would like you to talk to her just to be assured. Besides,” she added, “it will do Carmel good to talk to you.”

Nevertheless she made no move to find her daughter.

“You must forgive my pre-occupation,” she said. “From the moment we met I liked you. I felt you could be somebody in whom I could confide. Your concern for Carmel is touching —” She broke off at a tangent;

“You’re not married?”

“No.” I was surprised by her question.

“You look startled,” she said, smiling. “Please don’t think I’m a scheming mother. You see, Carmel can never marry, but I would like her to have the companionship of people nearer her own age. I feel she needs to talk to people now and again — particularly people who would understand her and her ways.”

I was bewildered by this turn in the conversation.

“What is the matter with her?” I asked.

“She’s different from other girls, in that her mind works differently. People who don’t understand her would perhaps think that she was a little deranged.”

THE FOUR AGES OF WOMAN

I remember the day I grew up.

I was fourteen and travelling alone on a bus to my first job. As I stepped inside I heard a mother say to her small son, "Stand up, Johnnie, and let the young lady sit down." She was referring to me!

The second milestone came when, after my marriage, a shopkeeper called me "Missus."

The third came when, after a difficult birth, a nurse put my firstborn into my arms saying, "Wake up, Mother . . ."

Alas, the fourth milestone in my life came last autumn.

I'm now sixty, but I still enjoy an occasional swim. Though the day was chilly, I went down to the beach. I pulled my bathing cap over my grey hair and prepared to enter the sea.

A young couple were at the tideline, the husband very reluctant to enter the cold water. As I plunged in I heard his wife say:

"Go on, Harry . . . if that old lady can go in, surely you can."

I recalled the white, shocked face of the girl I had almost injured the day before. Her curious immobility acquired a new significance in my mind.

“In what way is she not like other people?” I asked.

The woman pondered her reply a long time. “Sometimes she does very wild things,” she said finally.

“Take yesterday — running around the grounds and almost getting herself run over. Other times I hear her wandering round the house.

She will go on walking until I come to her and then she is quite calm and happy again.

"She is a free creature by nature. It would break her heart to be confined in any way."

Her attention was attracted by something outside the window.

"She's in the garden now. Why don't you go and talk to her?"

As I moved to the window, she said:

"Come back and have some tea before you go. I suppose in a sense you are now our family doctor."

OUTSIDE, Carmel was standing by my car. She wore a loose sweater and slacks and as I walked towards her I was struck by her resemblance to her mother.

"Hello," I said.

She lifted her gaze to me and, momentarily, beyond to the window behind me. She didn't appear surprised to see me.

"I thought I'd stop by," I explained, "to make sure you were all right."

"I'm quite well, thank you," she said slowly.

"I'm relieved to see you looking so well," I said. The conversation was tending to dry up and I was determined to stay awhile. "Your mother told me you've moved here quite recently," I started again.

"Yes," she said.

I looked around at the untidy grounds and wondered what I could say about it. When I turned my head she was smiling, a sympathetic smile that was all for me.

"It's dreadful, isn't it?" she said quietly.

"It could be lovely again," I said. "I'd like you to show me round. The house is a wonderful example of Georgian architecture."

She laughed outright at my floundering, a clear natural laugh without a shred of derision and it was a joy to hear.

"Forgive me," she said. "I won't show you the house because I'd be ashamed, but I will show you the gardens."

As we walked I noticed that unruly nature had encroached on every path and walk.

Only by the stream which meandered through the bottom of the garden was there a certain placid beauty.

We stopped here. It was the end of the tour. She sat down on a fallen tree.

"Well, what do you think of the place?"

I eluded her question. "It's very lovely here."

"I come here quite often," she said. "It's very peaceful."

Then, quite suddenly, she asked: "What do you think of Mother?"

"She's very lovely," I said without hesitation.

"She is indeed," Carmel said. "Mother is the most beautiful person I've ever known. She misses Shelton as a setting."

"Shelton?" I asked.

"Shelton was where we lived near Edinburgh." She sighed. "It was so different from this place."

"You miss it, too," I said. It was a half-question and she ignored it.

"Did Mother tell you to talk to me?"

I was taken aback by her directness. "Not exactly. After all, I came to see you."

"Did she tell you I was different?"

"Yes," I said, "but that is obvious."

She looked at me quickly.

"I mean, you're very lovely," I said.

Her eyes held mine for a moment and the colour tinged her cheeks. She looked away from me.

"It's so long since anybody told me that. It's nice to hear it."

"I wasn't being polite," I said.

"I know. Did Mother tell you I was deranged?"

"No," I said.

She smiled disconsolately. "She believes me to be a wild, deranged creature that needs constant vigilance and attention.

"She would sacrifice her life for me. She came here to give me scope for my tantrums and she would die rather than see me institutionalised."

I was shaken by her frankness, and while I groped for words she went on:

"As a doctor you could be interested in my case," she said, and for the first time there was cynicism in her voice.

"You sound and act perfectly normal to me," I said.

"Aren't these symptoms?" she asked, looking so disconsolate I longed to take her in my arms.

"I would like to be your friend," I said. "If I can help in any way —"

"There's nothing anybody can do," she cut in. "I've been gone too long!"

She came to her feet and without a word went up towards the house. After a moment she began to run, her long hair streaming behind her.

I followed more slowly, and when I reached the car the french windows were shut. I remembered I had been invited to stay to tea but the closed window seemed to cancel that.

As I sat behind the wheel of my car the front door opened and Carmel's mother appeared. She came down the three steps as if she floated over them.

"I was hoping you might have tea before you left," she said, "but under the circumstances we'd better make it another day. I'm very grateful you called."

I didn't know what to say.

"Thank you for talking to Carmel," she continued. "I'm sure she was pleased."

"She's a beautiful girl," I said. "She's different in that respect."

"She is very lovely," the woman said. "I must go to her now."

She didn't look back on her way to the door and I drove away immediately, the knowledge that I had a lead on what I considered a tragic mystery sending me rocketing down the drive.

I HAD a contact in Edinburgh. Kenneth Grahame and I had been students together and I knew where his practice was.

I phoned him that evening. Even as I heard his voice on the other end of the line I realised I could present him with very poor leads to the information I wanted.

All I had was the name "Shelton" and very little else. I was not encouraged by his reaction when I'd finished speaking.

"This is a big city, Keith. However, I'll see what I can do. If you don't hear from me in a couple of days you can forget it."

I was saddened by his pessimism but there was nothing more I could add to what I had already told him.

During the next four days the general health of Kilmel and the surrounding country took a slight turn for the worse. I was so busy that the problems of Howard House receded in my mind.

However, one evening on my way back to the village I made a detour to call on Carmel. I found the gates closed, a new chain and padlock welding them together.

I drove to the village completely despondent.

I found a letter from Kenneth Grahame waiting for me at the surgery. I read it over three times.

With the memory of the closed gates still in my mind I was saddened by the possibility that his information had come too late.

Then, suddenly, I was alarmed by the possibilities suggested by his letter.

I drove back down the lane, slowly cruising the length of the tall rubble wall that shut off the house. The trees towered from behind the wall, pressing against it so closely that the masonry bulged outwards in places.

In one such spot the stones had collapsed to a depth of three feet from the top. I got out of the car and lifted myself up through the gap.

I had a dozen or so scratches before I came out on a fallow field. I walked back parallel to the wall until I came to the drive and then approached the house.

My heart sank when I saw it. It looked utterly deserted and the windows reflecting the reddening sky gave it a sinister air.

Where the drive met the gravelled frontage I caught a movement behind the house where the land fell away towards the stream.

Even as I did, the french windows opened and Mrs Stuart stood there, motionless, still holding the leaves of the window apart like an actress holding the curtains on stage.

I could not tell by her expression if she was glad to see me. She was very pale and there were visible shadows beneath her eyes. Though her features were drawn, still her beauty clung to her, only now it was a tragic beauty.

THE DAY I STOOD

IT happened in the Sixties, when the first accommodation block designed for the Women's Royal Naval Service was built at H.M.S. Ariel, Leigh-on-Solent. H.R.H. Princess Marina, Duchess of Kent, was invited to perform the naming ceremony.

The Royal Navy likes these occasions to go really smoothly and so there are rehearsals, carefully timed.

For the final one a person representing Princess Marina was needed and I was chosen to be her stand-in.

I was petrified! However, once I was attired in a smart summer coat, matching shoes and gloves and a most regal flowery hat, I began to feel more confident.

My "lady-in-waiting" and I were taxied round the perimeter track of the airfield in a real aircraft. The Admiral stepped forward and saluted and then introduced me to the captain of H.M.S. Ariel and other officers.

I said something suitable to each, which was fun as I knew them all, of course. Then I found myself in a shiny black car with the Admiral.

Even for the rehearsal, the route was lined with airmen. The Admiral was busy saluting so I did what I hoped was a gracious royal slow wave!

At the Wardroom there were more introductions and after pretending to sign a Visitors' Book I was asked if I wished to "retire."

I spent a very genuine penny,

thereby assisting the timing of the rehearsal no end!

I was escorted to the spot where I had to take the Royal Salute. That was the worst part. I felt very uncertain inside and so very alone standing there.

The officer bearing the Queen's Colour was enormously tall and made me feel deliciously tiny, like the Queen Mother. They presented arms

---

We stood looking at each other for a moment.

"The gates were locked," I said. "I was worried."

"Of course." Her lips scarcely moved.

"I didn't know if you had gone away."

"We are going soon," she said. "I think we must go now."

Her hands fell away from the window frames. "Please come in."

With a premonition of disaster heavily upon me I followed her into the room. She stood in the centre of it, her hands clasped in front of her.

IN FOR ROYALTY

and the National Anthem was played, whilst the Colour was dipped in front of me.

Then the officer of the Guard marched over with the grimmest face I'd ever seen (I think he was scared, too) and invited me to inspect the Guard.

The band was playing softly as I walked slowly down the first rank and back along the second. I stopped occasionally to ask a man how long he'd been in the navy or what his job was.

BY now I was beginning to relax and rather enjoyed being on the other end of an inspection. I enquired most kindly what work my own typist did. Very unfair really — she had a terrible time keeping a straight face!

There were more presentations before the naming ceremony and then a voice which didn't sound a bit like mine said, "I name this building Princess Marina Block" and I pulled a tassel which parted some makeshift curtains to reveal an engraved notice giving details of the naming.

Then I was presented with a bouquet of very plastic flowers.

A tour of the new block followed and in each room officers and wrens were present to make conversation, if required.

The First Officer introduced them to me and they curtseyed and called me "Your Royal Highness."

The Admiral created great alarm by leaving the planned route and putting his head round the door of a cabin which was not at all ready for inspection. Its occupants had obviously had a rush to get on parade in time, for working uniforms lay on the beds and dressing-tables were not particularly neat.

"That looks much more fun" he remarked happily, before being persuaded back to the proper route.

The wrens gave three really rousing cheers ("Give a good yell — it's nearly over") as I climbed the steps to the aircraft, turned, waved and smiled. Inside, I sank down thankfully and found that I was sitting on that plastic bouquet thoughtfully placed on the seat by someone!

It had been a really memorable experience and certainly one which I will never forget. ■

by PAT HOLDEN

"When I suggested you talk to Carmel I made a very grave mistake." She lifted her hand to stop me speaking. "I don't blame you. It was my fault.

"I had forgotten how sensitive and impressionable Carmel can be. Ever since you've been here she has changed. I think she believes herself to be in love with you."

"Is that bad?" I said gently.

"Under normal circumstances it would be a wonderful thing." Mrs Stuart moved across the room and added with her back turned to me:

"But, for Carmel, who is already emotionally disturbed, it could be disastrous."

She turned. "There was no doubting her concern. "I haven't been quite honest with you about my daughter. I told you she was different, but that was only a half-truth. The whole truth is that she is mentally ill.

"She's getting better, of course — at least she was until she spoke to you. I thought the companionship of people other than myself would help her. Now I see I was wrong. That is why I had the gates locked."

She touched the scar on her forehead and my glance followed her fingers.

"How did that happen, Mrs Stuart?" I asked.

She took her hand away quickly and frowned. Then she sighed.

"It was unfortunate. But it serves to remind me of the gradual improvement in Carmel. She has never attempted to do anything like it since — and that was four years ago."

I looked at her in horror. "Carmel did that?"

She made an impatient gesture with her hand. "It was Carmel's hand but, of course, not Carmel. She didn't know what she was doing at the time."

"What did she use?" I asked.

Mrs Stuart smiled. "I don't know. When I regained consciousness she refused to tell me where it was. I was so afraid for her that I never mentioned it again, not to anyone until now.

"I've also kept her condition a secret. She was such a free spirit that any sort of confinement would destroy her."

She looked haggard in a moment. The transformation was alarming. "I think I'll lie down now, Dr Lindsay. If you'll excuse me . . ."

I turned at the french windows and she waited for my question.

"Where is Mr Stuart, your husband?"

Her eyes widened for a moment and then a sad smile touched her lips.

"You have a genius for unearthing skeletons, Dr Lindsay," she said wearily. "My husband left me a long time ago."

"I'm sorry," I said and went outside.

I DID not go down the drive. Instead, as soon as I reached the corner of the house, I turned towards the stream. I didn't particularly mind if Mrs Stuart saw me.

I followed the overgrown path until it came to the stream and here in the deepening twilight I found Carmel seated on the fallen tree.

She didn't look up as I approached nor did she move as I sat down beside her. Her long hair screened her face from me.

"Shelton must be a wonderful place," I said. "A friend of mine described it to me recently."

She lifted her head and swept her hair behind her shoulder. She looked at me then with a quiet regard.

"He explained to me," I went on, "that the property is now vacant following a tragic motor accident in which the owner died. His daughter and wife were lucky to escape with their lives. The mother sustained what were considered minor injuries . . . a few bruises and a deep cut in her forehead."

She shivered and I covered her hands with mine. They were icy.

"I suspect," I said, "that your mother's injury was not as minor as was supposed. She is quite ill."

"I know," said Carmel tonelessly. "She believes that I am the one who needs medical care and as a consequence she is distracted with worry.

"It's a tragic-comedy really since our convictions compel us to follow each other around all the time. I love her very much. She's a wonderful woman, you know."

"And she cares for you," I said. I could see that her eyes were soft and brimming with tears.

"I know that. It's a great love indeed that overcomes the conviction that I once tried to kill her. This was why after the accident she wouldn't speak.

"She insisted on leaving the hospital lest she betray me. We've been moving ever since. Daddy's death turned her mind."

"I don't believe she knows what happened to your father," I said gently. "Although I have no way of being absolutely sure, I believe she remembers nothing of the accident, except perhaps you bending over her — did you do this?"

Carmel's hands stirred under mine. "Yes, of course — when she was on the road."

"This is probably where the suspicion you had struck her was born," I said.

She shivered again and I put my arm about her and lifted her to her feet.

"We can't have you catching cold. I think your mother is going to be quite well once she has attention. We'll have another look at that scar of hers and see what's going on beneath it."

I led her away from the stream, my arm still round her waist and she leaned against me. Some distance from the house I saw her mother waiting for us. She looked anxious and distraught.

"Poor Mother!" Carmel whispered.

I tightened my arm around her and smiled reassuringly. "Don't worry, Carmel. You're no longer alone."

When we came up to Mrs Stuart we stopped. She smiled gently at me.

"You found her," she said.

"I did," I said, "and she will never be lost again."

I held out my hand to Carmel's mother and she took it like a child. We walked slowly back to the house.

— * THE END * —

I NEVER meant to harm our Sally when I came up with ideas for getting rid of her. You see, it started this way.

There's me, Nigel Aimes, twelve years old and an "ideas man." Then there's my brothers, Christopher, nine, and William, seven and a bit. Sally is nineteen and not bad looking. She's pretty decent — for a sister.

Anyhow, what started it all was when Dad got a bonus at work and bought us this super racing track and all the cars to go with it. It's terrific except you needs lots of room to lay out the whole track.

At first Mum let us use the dining-room and it was great until one of the cars hurtled off the track and smashed a pane in the french windows.

Mum was cross and told us we couldn't use it downstairs again and that we'd have to set it up in one of our bedrooms. The trouble was that it was too big for our rooms. So we measured up Sally's and, guess what? It was perfect.

I went and asked Mum if Sally would swop with me but Mum refused point-blank.

She wouldn't give me a reason. She just looked as if she was far away and seeing things that bothered her.

Well, I could tell it was no good arguing with her, so me, Christopher and William held a conference in my bedroom. I told the other two straight.

"We've got to get rid of Sally."

GETTING RID OF

Complete Story by
JANE O'HARE

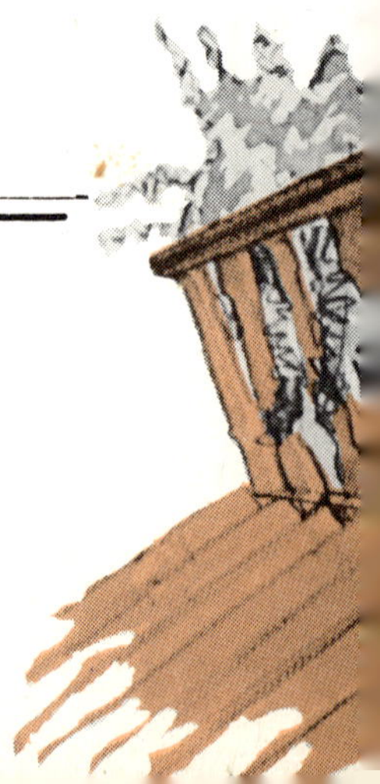

Our Sally was a good sister, as sisters go. And, as sisters go — she went!

William can be stupid sometimes. “You mean kill her?” He gulped and turned all white-faced.

“Don’t be so daft. Nigel doesn’t mean murder. They hang you for that,” Christopher said scornfully.

“You’re both wrong,” I told them. “I didn’t mean murder her. After all, she is our sister and we love her even when she’s rotten. And they don’t hang you for murder. They stick you in prison.”

Of course we had an argument about loving her, but I soon made them get down to business. By business, I mean I came up with the ideas for shifting Sally and then we all decided which was the best way.

My first idea was creepy-crawlies and ghosts.

William looked scared but he agreed, and Christopher was quite excited. I told them that if it didn’t work we’d try getting her a job as far away from home as possible.

But that might be difficult. Sally'd been working at the advertising agency for eight months now, and that was the longest she'd ever stayed in a job since she'd left school at seventeen.

My third idea was the hardest.

"We could try and get her married. Quick."

Of course William asked who to and Christopher said glumly that the only decent boy she'd brought home had been Alex Saunders, a photographer, and she'd fallen out with him.

All the rest had been lousy. He was right, too.

Anyway, we decided on the code-name, G.S.O. — "Getting Sally Out." I wanted to put our plots into full-scale operation right away, but the other two wanted to try them one at a time. So we had a vote and I lost.

"OK," I said. "We'll do the creepy-crawlies and ghosts first."

"Don't do too much of the ghosts," William pleaded. " 'Cos I'm scared of them, and Sally might be, too."

"It's got to be as scary as possible," I told him bluntly, "or it won't work. It won't scare you because you're in on it. Now, this is how we'll start."

I'VE watched lots of horror films on TV and read heaps of ghost books. The best ones are where they really build up the tension or something.

One story I read was about a man who was dead scared of spiders.

"Spiders first," I ordered. "The real thing. Not the imitation sort because that would give the game away."

It was easy to get hold of some beauties from the shed and the garden.

We gathered at night in my bedroom. Just before Sally went to get washed, I whipped into the bathroom, put the plug in the bath, and put a smashing hairy spider in.

We put another one very carefully in the soapholder under the soap. Then we went to our bedrooms just in case anyone got suspicious.

Spider One, in the bath, started things off nicely. There was a screech from Sally that almost frightened us. I lay in the dark and heard Mum and Dad hurrying along the landing.

Dad soon got rid of Spider One and all was quiet except for Sally splashing about. Her next screech, at Spider Two, was really blood curdling.

Again Mum and Dad went to her. I could hear murmuring and when they came out Dad said, "I couldn't see any spider. I've searched everywhere."

He sounded quite annoyed at Sally, which was strange. He isn't usually like that.

Next morning at breakfast Sally looked as if she hadn't slept well, but there was something else about her that bothered me. I told the others about it when we met in my bedroom after school.

"Did either of you notice how jumpy Sally was at breakfast?" I asked.

They both nodded and William said hopefully that maybe we wouldn't need ghosts after all, only spiders.

I shook my head. "No. We can't use spiders again. Dad's sure to guess if we do."

Christopher was frowning. "Nigel," he said, "it wasn't only Sally who was jumpy — Mum and Dad were ever so quiet. You don't think we've frightened them as well?"

I shook my head. "No. It's something more than that but I can't think what." After another deep think I added, "As a matter of fact

A Sacrifice Worth Making

NOT far from where I live there's a beautiful garden. One of its main features is a magnificent privet hedge. I happen to know the hedge is also the owner's pride and joy.

I can remember when he planted it, and over the years I've stopped for a chat and seen the hedge grow and thicken.

That's why I was so surprised the other day to see him with a hedge trimmer, lopping two feet off the top of it!

I could see immediately it was no pruning job and, being naturally curious, I just had to ask the reason. I knew he'd have to have a good one — and he did!

The weekend before, he told me, he'd had a surprise visit from his next-door neighbour. He used the word "surprise" because his neighbour, Miss Blake, is a lady in her late seventies who generally keeps very much to herself. Or so he thought.

Very hesitantly she'd told him that, being bothered with arthritis, she didn't get about so well these days.

It was a great comfort to her, she'd said, to be able to glance into his front garden occasionally. She liked to see him and his wife working there and watch his three young children playing.

Recently, his hedge had grown to a height that prevented her from doing this.

"She's a proud old girl," he said. "It took a lot of courage to come and see me."

And so, he was cutting his beloved hedge.

"It's the least I can do," he said. "It not only means she can keep an eye on us, we'll be able to keep any eye on her."

It's a heartwarming story, but it made me wonder — just how many of us have a Miss Blake living next door to us?

I've been wondering if Sally hasn't quarrelled with Mum and Dad lately. They don't talk and laugh like they used to."

Christopher suggested that they might all be extra tired, but I was doubtful.

"I don't think so," I said. "It's more than that. I'd bet my last ten pence on it. Ah well, Operation G.S.O., Phase 2, must be launched as soon as there's a good breeze. Prepared?"

They nodded.

We had it all worked out. One of us had to climb a ladder and rig up a piece of scratchy shrub that would scrape and tap at Sally's window.

Because of the risk I would do it. William could hold the ladder and Christopher would keep watch, just in case we were caught. I threatened them both. Whatever happened, we must not get caught or all future plots were doomed.

"There's no wind tonight," William said, sounding relieved.

So we waited. It was several nights later before a good wind came. We were lucky, too, because it was a Friday. That's the day Mum goes to see Aunt Cis and leaves our tea. Also it's the day Sally stays on in town to go out with her latest boyfriend.

We hadn't met him and didn't want to, even if she had gone out with him longer than the others. He couldn't be another Alex, that was asking the impossible. As for Dad, he never gets home before seven o'clock.

It wasn't all that easy, I can tell you, climbing that ladder in a strong breeze. I had to rig the shrub branch carefully in a position to scrape Sally's window. Once, I looked down and came over all funny but I made it.

It was strange, but there was still something bothering me quite a lot, and I knew it wasn't scaring Sally.

No, it was something else — something worse. Home just hadn't been the same for a couple of weeks, maybe longer, Mum and Dad didn't talk very much, and Sally was even quieter.

It couldn't be because of the spiders because I'd sort of noticed it before we started Operation G.S.O. I tried to ignore it. No doubt it was private, and me, Christopher and William respect privacy because we like it ourselves.

The piece of shrub was working well when we went up to check before the rest of the family came home. It was so effective that William went white as a ghost himself and *he* knew what it was!

WE'D had our tea and were doing our homework when Mum and Sally came in. Again I had that feeling that something was wrong.

Mum and Sally had red patches about their eyes, like they'd been crying, and there seemed to be a sort of tug-of-war between them, only without the rope, if you know what I mean?

At supper-time it was the same, Mum and Dad kept exchanging

glances and Sally hardly ate anything. Still, if something was wrong, what could we do about it?

All the same, I began to feel so rotten inside that I was tempted to tell the others and call tonight's "haunting" off. I couldn't do it, though, or they'd have thought me chicken.

Before going to bed we took solemn vows to stay awake, so that we'd know if Phase 2 was working. The wind howled about the house, getting worse as the night became darker. Surely that shrub was still working?

But time went on and on and nothing happened until around two in the morning. I'd tossed and turned and got hotter and hotter until at last I had to fling the bedclothes off me and sit up. It was then I heard Sally crying.

When she and Alex had fallen out Sally had sobbed something awful, but this was different.

I can't explain properly, but it was more than I could stand. True, we wanted her room but we never meant to *hurt* her and those crying sounds showed she *was* hurt, bad.

In seconds I was out of bed and fetched the other two. Outside Sally's door I whispered to them to listen.

After a minute William said, very quietly, "Nigel! Please, we didn't mean to make her cry like that. Let's go and tell her."

Christopher agreed, so I tapped on Sally's door and when there was no answer we all went in. Sally's bedside lamp was on and she lay huddled under the clothes. The shrub was still working but I was certain, somehow, that she wasn't listening.

"Sally?" I said softly. "Listen, it isn't really a ghost, it was us because we wanted your bedroom for our racing car set."

She peeped at me from beneath the clothes and then at Christopher and William, and she swallowed hard.

"Wh-what ghosts, Nigel?"

While I explained, telling about the spiders as well, she sat up and rolled over to get a tissue and blew her nose.

Then she shook her head at us. "Believe me, I'm not crying because of anything you've done."

She hesitated. "I'm upset because Mum and Dad don't understand something that's very important to me. We've argued about it for nearly three weeks and I don't believe they'll see my point of view now. So, I'm leaving home."

We looked at each other and, though we should have been pleased, none of us were. William looked like he'd burst out crying himself any moment.

"Tell us about it, Sally," I pleaded. "Please? Maybe we can't help but telling us won't do any harm, will it?"

She gulped, nodded, and said, "I don't suppose you remember Alex. He was a photographer. Still is, but last year we — we fell out . . ."

Continued on page 37

THE OLD GIRL'S HOUR OF GLORY

It was an old-fashioned, run-down taxi-cab, but for its owner and a young couple about to begin married life it made that special day one they would always remember.

by MARGARET O'REILLY

BEFORE my marriage I worked in an office above the main street of a small market town. In those days cows out-numbered cars and life flowed by at a gentle pace!

Opposite the window where I sat at my typewriter was a little black-and-white cottage, and in slack moments I found myself following the daily lives of the occupants — a little Irish taxi-driver, his wife and two children.

I could always tell when the taxi was booked for a wedding! The day before the occasion was

devoted entirely to making the car worthy of what its owner clearly felt to be an honour.

The whole family played their part. The cottage only had one downstairs room, so I could see right in as the mother washed a long length of white satin ribbon and dried it in front of the fire, turning it carefully from time to time.

Next, with an ironing board placed near the window — she liked to see what was going on, too — she would iron the ribbon with loving care,

While she was busy with the ribbon, Father and his teenage son would clean and polish the taxi from top to bottom. The little girl, having removed the pieces of carpet from the inside, would spread them out on the cobbles and brush them vigorously.

Only when every inch of the little biscuit-tin type car had passed the most meticulous examination was it covered carefully with a tarpaulin to await the final touch — the putting in place of the ribbon.

This special task was the wife's and was left to the very last minute, so that the bow and the long fluttering streamers looked absolutely fresh and perfect when the little man proudly took his seat behind the wheel and set off on his romantic mission.

One day during my lunch hour I got into conversation with him, and told him how I enjoyed watching them all preparing for a wedding.

To my surprise his face fell.

"I do my best," Mick said with a shrug, "but I only get Registry Office weddings. Sure there's not the same romance about them! It's church weddings I'd like to be doing — or chapel, of course!" he added hastily.

"But why do you only get Registry Office weddings?" I asked.

"Ah, well," he explained, "they're smaller affairs entirely.

"I've only the one taxi and it's no size at all. To do a proper wedding I'd have to be going back and forth ever so many times. People won't be bothered with the like o' that.

"Besides," he added, "they want them long limousines. My poor old girl's not good enough! No, it's Registry Office weddings for me till the day I retire!"

"Mick," I said impulsively, "if I get married in this town I promise — I absolutely promise, that I'll book your taxi for my wedding!"

He grabbed my hands.

"It's a bargain!" he cried eagerly. "For you I'll do the old girl up a treat! Don't forget now!"

I felt a bit guilty. Oh, I'd meant what I'd said . . . but the fact remained that the odds were not in favour of my being married in the town. I lived in digs, my real home was far away, and in any case I hadn't even got a steady boyfriend!

But unexpected situations arise!

WAR broke out, bringing with it difficulties in transport and the stern slogan "Is Your Journey Really Necessary?"

I met my future husband, a handsome young serviceman stationed in the town, and we decided it would be simpler to be married there.

Wedding breakfasts in hotels and restaurants were not officially allowed, though this restriction was sometimes evaded by putting two or three tables together.

Even so, numbers had to be limited, and as not many of our relatives could face the long cold train journey, we reckoned that we would have only about ten people in all.

A small wedding maybe — but it would be in church. I went across and made the arrangements with Mick. He looked solemnly at me.

"I won't forget it!" he assured me huskily.

Unfortunately, from that moment the numbers rocketed upwards! People decided they could make it after all. The manager of the restaurant where we had booked our modest reception unearthed a legal loophole by which he could cater for quite a few extra bodies. However, we soon realised that one small taxi simply wasn't going to be enough for all our "extra" guests.

It was really my fiancé's family I was worried about. What would they think? With some trepidation I broached the subject. In view of the increased numbers, I asked my fiancé if we should pay Mick double and ask to be released from our booking?

Sometimes, in those whirlwind wartimes romances, the couple didn't really know each other very well. I don't think we did, till then.

My fiancé looked steadily at me.

"What sort of a marriage would we have, love," he asked me gently, "if we started off by hurting someone?"

I knew, then, that we'd make it together.

WE were married on a bitterly cold February morning. The day before my wedding, I watched the familiar ritual being performed — this time for me!

Most of the guests had stayed the night in a local hotel, and Mick had to pick them up in relays, starting very, very early indeed! The first batch must have sat shivering in the unheated church for well over an hour by the time I arrived, six or seven trips later!

Some of the guests who lived locally had walked to the church, but we didn't want them to have to walk to the reception, too, so that meant even more journeys for the taxi unless we could cram in as many as possible on each run. This we did.

So instead of my husband and myself driving off together in dignified state, the bridesmaids, best man and several assorted guests all bundled in with us, sitting on each other's laps with total lack of ceremony.

I saw one or two of the guests raising their eyebrows, obviously thinking that we either didn't know how things ought to be done or were trying to do it on the cheap, but we didn't care!

To crown everything, Mick's wife had appeared on the scene in apron and slippers, and occupied the front passenger seat together with their mongrel dog, thus taking up precious space, but it all added to the hilarity!

Back and forth, back and forth, the "old girl" staggered, zig-zagging alarmingly at times, as Mick, who was in roaring high spirits, turned round to laugh and joke with his passengers.

We asked him to bring his wife into the reception for a drink, but he couldn't. He had another wedding — "one of them Registry Office affairs" — to fit in before picking us up again to take us to the station.

"But I don't mind now," he told us with a wide grin. "I'll never mind any more. Me and the 'old girl' have had our hour of glory!" And with a toot from the horn, he drove off, the happiest man in the world. ■

Continued from page 33

"Yes! You cried a lot then," Christopher put in. "It got on my nerves and I used to wonder how much water you had inside you to let out."

Sally smiled, just a little bit. "I'm sorry. But I loved him. I still do love him. That's why I'm so happy at the agency. You see, he works there and — and we'd like to be married, but Mum and Dad aren't pleased about it because they said Alex hurt me once and may do again.

"I can't make them see that Alex had to be sure he loved me, really loved me, first. He didn't realise he was hurting me. Also he needed a better salary and a permanent job. He's sure he loves me now and his salary is better but Mum and Dad are still against him."

"You're old enough to marry without Mum and Dad saying yes or no," I pointed out wisely.

Sally nodded. "Oh, yes, but I love them, too, in a different way, and I'd like them to meet Alex again. I'm sure they'd agree he's changed."

"Alex's the only fellow you've brought home we ever liked," I put in. "I'm an ideas man, Sally. Let me think about it. I'll come up with something."

She managed to smile at us before we trooped back to our bedrooms without even saying goodnight to each other. We all felt ashamed. I lay awake for ages, thinking hard, but I couldn't come up with a single idea.

NEXT morning when the others asked me what to do, I told them straight. All I could think of was being honest and telling Mum and Dad we knew about Alex, liked him a lot, and would they give him and Sally a chance?

So that's what happened. I was spokesman and I told the lot. All about Operation G.S.O. as well, and I told them they'd be wrong if they thought we were only pretending we liked Alex because Sally might marry him and then we could have her bedroom.

Believe it or not, when I'd finished speaking Mum and Dad suddenly burst out laughing.

Dad said, "If you three like Alex that much we'd better give him a chance." His eyes were still twinkling from laughing when he added, "If we don't, I can see you starting Operation G.M.D.O!"

When I asked him what that was he grinned and said, "It's short for 'Getting Mum and Dad Out'!"

You know something? Honesty pays, just like they say. Alex and Sally are getting married next month and moving into a flat. I'm having Sally's room as soon as they're married and living happily ever after — like they say in those sloppy romance stories.

*** THE END ***

A Promise Is A Promise

She was happily married. She had three wonderful children. But ten years ago she made a promise to meet a special man at a special place . . .

Complete Story
by ISOBEL STEWART

HE wouldn't remember, Beth James thought sadly. Ten years ago is a long time.

It was unreasonable and unrealistic to think that he would remember the promise made by a boy of twenty and a girl of nineteen.

"Ten years from now, we'll come back. Wherever we are, whatever we're doing, we'll come back here."

He had held both her hands in his and looked down at her then, his eyes holding hers steadily, before he kissed her.

"That's for goodbye," he'd said shakily. "Goodbye, and — good luck."

"Goodbye, and good luck," she had echoed.

And then, hand in hand, they had run down the hill, run until they were laughing and breathless, the awkwardness and the sudden uncertainty of that moment gone.

"I'm sure we're right," she had said again, earnestly, as they walked along the river bank on the way home.

"Of course we are," he had agreed, swinging her hand. "Look, Beth — we've known each other since you were sixteen. All right, we get on well together, we — we're fond of each other, but neither of us has had the chance to know anyone else."

"We haven't wanted to," she had reminded him honestly. And then, taking her hand away from his — "Anyway, there's lots more we're going to do with our lives than . . . than marriage."

He had been silent for a while, making no attempt to take her hand in his again.

"But we'll come back, ten years from now," he had reminded her. "When I'm a Harley Street specialist, and your name is in lights in the West End. And we can see if we've changed our minds about — about anything."

He hadn't kissed her again, and when they reached her gate they had said goodbye — solemnly, seriously. The next day, he had left for a summer job near his university, and a few weeks later she had gone to drama school.

And now, ten years later, Beth stood in her sunny kitchen and remembered that promise . . .

Soon it would be the first of August. An easy day to remember.

But why should he remember, after all?

It was different for a woman, she thought, putting the baby's bottle in the jug to heat. A woman had time to remember as she went about the sameness of her everyday life.

A woman could be washing nappies, feeding a baby, fetching children from school, clearing up supper, and all the time she could be remembering a boy she had known and loved ten years ago.

And wondering if he remembered the girl she had been when she was nineteen.

At first, as the time drew nearer, she told herself that she wouldn't go. Better not to risk the hurt of finding out for certain that he hadn't remembered, or worse perhaps, that he had remembered, and — hadn't managed to find time, because he hadn't thought it mattered.

One way or the other, she told herself more than once, it would be better not to know.

But more and more in these last days of July she found herself thinking about him, and longing, desperately, to know that he had remembered.

Even to know that he had forgotten, she thought, would be better than uncertainty. Then she could come to terms with it, and accept completely how foolish she had been to think he would remember.

If he has forgotten, she told herself, as she lifted the baby and sat down to give him his bottle, then I'll just go on doing all the things I do, I'll be grateful for what I have. A happy marriage, three lovely children, a nice home — I'm one of the lucky ones.

And yet, she had to be honest with herself, honest enough to admit that she needed more than that. She needed the certainty that the boy she had loved ten years ago had remembered their promise.

CAREFULLY, as the day came nearer, she made her plans. The two little girls would go to their grandmother's from school. The baby would go to Sandra, her friend and neighbour, as they often helped each other out. Sandra was a good friend, Beth often thought with gratitude. A friend who understood so much that could never be said.

And there should be no problem with her husband. He didn't come home on Thursdays for lunch. She would be home, she told herself, long before he came back in the evening. He need never know.

It was only on the morning of the first that Beth began to feel guilty. The baby had been restless, and she had been up a few times with him, so that in the morning she didn't hear the alarm clock.

When she awoke, it was to find her husband putting a cup of tea down beside her.

"Sorry, love," he said, kissing her cheek, "but Mandy can't find her spelling book, and it's almost time for them to go to school. Can you help us?"

Beth sat up, rubbing her eyes.

"You shouldn't have let me sleep." And then, with the ability that had come over the years to function on more than one level — "She left her spelling book in the kitchen, it's on top of the fridge."

Quickly she drank her tea and got out of bed, pulling on slacks and shirt. When she got to the kitchen, Mandy and Sue were putting their blazers on. She cleaned the egg from Mandy's mouth, and tied the ribbons on Sue's pigtails.

"Daddy gave us breakfast," Sue told her. "And he ate my egg because I didn't want it."

"I'll be watching to see that you eat your egg tomorrow, then," Beth replied, kissing her daughters and waving goodbye to them.

In the kitchen, she poured more tea for both of them. "Steven's still asleep," he told her. "I didn't disturb him."

"Fine, I'll leave him as long as possible. Poor baby, it's that back tooth, I'm sure." She hesitated, and then, casually, she said — "You won't be in for lunch, of course?"

"No, you know I never am on Thursdays."

He looked at his watch then, and said he would be late. But as she stood at the door saying goodbye to him, it seemed to her that he was deliberately putting off time, mentioning things that could have waited for another time.

Suddenly contrite, she put her arms around his neck and kissed him. "Try not to be late tonight," she murmured.

"I'll try," he promised, as he so often did.

WHEN he had gone, the house seemed strangely quiet with the baby still asleep. She needn't go until later, for if he came, it would be at midday. If he came . . .

She made beds, and dusted and vacuumed, and when the baby woke she dressed him and gave him his breakfast. Then putting him in his pram, she wheeled him around to the garden next door before coming back to the kitchen to put the kettle on for coffee.

We never used to think of things like coffee, she thought, remembering, as she filled the flask. We took apples with us and sometimes we made a fire and cooked sausages on sticks. But now I'm filling a flask with coffee, enough for two, and packing some sandwiches. The years of domesticity have changed me.

But the memory of her husband letting her sleep and waking her with a cup of tea was still with her. She smiled a little as she thought of the girl who would walk miles with only an apple to eat, changing so much.

With her flask and sandwiches in a basket, she set off, and it was strange not to be carrying a bottle for the baby or juice for the little girls. Strange to have no load of nappies, no extra shorts and socks in case of any emergencies.

Strange to be alone and myself again, Beth thought, as she reached the bank of the river.

It had changed, of course, in the ten years. Then, there had been no houses anywhere near and now there was a housing estate coming right up to the bank where they had so often walked hand in hand. She had known this, of course, but somehow it was different, seeing it all so close.

But the river itself hadn't changed, and as she walked along beside it, brown and sparkling on its bed of stones, she thought that she must bring the children here. Usually, at the weekend, if they did have time to go anywhere, they went to the beach, but it would be nice to bring them to the river sometimes.

Where the river widened into a deep pool, they used to swim.

At first, a whole group of them, noisy and laughing teenagers, the boys throwing the girls in, splashing them.

And then later, just the two of them, coming here on a summer evening when already the chill of the water made her shiver as she went in. She stood for a while looking down into the water, remembering.

Then she took the path up the hill, the path that led to the old oak tree at the top. This had been their special place, their secret place.

A Moment Of Pure Magic

IT was early morning and a chilly drizzle had kept most people indoors. The street was very quiet. In fact, I had it all to myself until an elderly lady came out from a house some fifty yards in front of me.

I didn't pay much attention to her at first. I was too intent on getting home and out of the wet as quickly as possible.

Then, quite suddenly, she stopped in her tracks and stared at the ground in front of her.

She's dropped something, I thought, and hurried to see if I could help.

But as I drew nearer, I could see what had caught her eyes. There, chalked on the pavement, were the numbered boxes of a hopscotch game.

Then it happened. She gave a quick glance around, and not having seen me, she went hopping and skipping down the boxes. Then, pausing for a moment to catch her breath, she went sedately on her way.

It was all over in a few seconds, but it was, for me, a moment of pure magic.

I laughed out loud but, believe me, I wasn't laughing at her. I felt privileged at having shared a little in what is often called a "mad impulse."

Mad? I don't think it was mad. In fact, I felt like catching her up and congratulating her.

I didn't, of course. It was a moment she deserved to have all to herself.

This was where he had kissed her for the first time, and where they had kissed goodbye, that day ten years ago.

HE wasn't there, but she knew that she was early. She sat down with her back against the trunk of the old tree. The summer sun was shining warm on her face, so she closed her eyes.

When she opened them, he was coming up the hill.

There was a moment of breathless shock as she realised that she had been so thoroughly immersed in the past that she had expected to see the boy he had been, instead of the man he had become in these ten years.

Then she stood up, and went towards him, slowly, unbelieving.

"You remembered," she whispered at last, as he stood looking down at her. "I didn't think you would."

"And I didn't think you would," he replied gravely. But his eyes were smiling, warm and smiling, as they always had been. He took her hand, just as he always had done and they went towards the tree.

"Coffee," he said with pleasure. "I'm sure you're a good and thoughtful wife, Beth."

The gentle teasing in his voice brought warm colour to her cheeks. "I hope so," she returned with spirit. "Because — because I've got a good and thoughtful husband."

She poured coffee for them both, and handed him his. His hand brushed hers as he took his cup, and her heart thudded unevenly.

"Tell me something, Beth," he said at last, quietly. "Have you no regrets about not being an actress — not having your name in lights in the West End?"

She thought about this before she answered.

"Sometimes," she admitted at last, slowly, honestly. "Sometimes I look around the kitchen, or I stop when I'm hanging out a line of nappies, and I think that once I wanted so much more from life than this."

She was silent for a moment, thinking of how to put it so that he would understand. "And then I watch my baby in his pram, waving his fat little hands in front of his face, or — or we come home late, and we go into the little girls' room and see them asleep. Or I wake up late, with a cup of tea beside me . . ."

She looked at him, anxious. Would he understand what she was saying?

"And you, Paul?" she asked, after a moment. "What about Harley Street?"

He shook his head. "Harley Street was never meant for me," he said with certainty. "I'm happier as an ordinary doctor."

He looked at her steadily. "With a wife and children who mean everything in the world to me."

She pulled a piece of grass, and looked down at it. "But if you hadn't married?" she asked. "Wouldn't you perhaps have — have done more?"

Continued on page 46

"Come On, Missu
Be A Sport!"

THERE I was, deck chair angled to catch the most sun, sipping a cup of tea and thinking deliciously of a little afternoon nap when a ball soared over my garden wall. I threw it back and settled down again.

Minutes later, it happened again— only this time the ball hit me! Again I entered into the spirit of things and threw it back.

Kids, I thought fondly. After all, I could hardly complain about other people's children when I had two little boys of my own, could I?

But my feeling didn't last long. Again and again the ball came over the wall — more often than not landing on me. I can tell you, when you're thinking pleasant drowsy thoughts it's more than a little disturbing!

As I got up to retrieve the ball for the umpteenth time I felt my eyes narrowing dangerously. Playing ball is all very well, I thought, as I grovelled among the rose bushes, but there's a limit!

I thought of my own children who were now playing cricket with their pals in the park — away from tired mothers, like me, who were trying to rest.

So why was I being persecuted by other people's inconsiderate offspring?

The ball was covered in mud, having cunningly landed in the dampest part of the rose bed, and as I wriggled out backwards I kept telling myself that boys will be boys!

I threw the ball back over the wall just as two heads began to appear over the top of it.

"Thanks, Missus," somebody said and I softened slightly. At least they had been taught basic manners somewhere along the line! Now surely they would realise that behind this wall was a kindly, tired lady trying to sleep.

I HAD just got to that stage when reality was beginning to merge with fantasy when — would you believe it — the ball landed neatly on my cup and splattered the contents over my feet.

It was too much!

I marched to the gate, swung it open and confronted the offenders.

The smaller one was about ten years old, with the face of a saint — pink cheeks, bright, innocent blue eyes, golden curls and a gentle, endearing smile on his rose-red lips.

The older boy was like a miniature Edward G. Robinson with a cynical twist to his mouth and eyes heavy with hostility.

"Now, look here," I said grimly. "What do you think you're doing?"

Angelface grinned, showing a most disarming gap in his top set of teeth. Edward G. frowned and, setting his hands on his hips, moved a step closer to me.

"Now, look here," I repeated

Playing the game is all very well, says Margaret Brown, but there comes a time when the referee has to step in and blow the whistle!

loudly, backing off slightly. "What do you think you're playing at?"

Angelface forgave me with a soft nod. "Tennith," he lisped, his smile never wavering.

It was quite unexpected and I faltered, "Well — well then — can't you play tennith, I mean tennis, somewhere else? Not in front of my house, do you understand? Or else I'll . . ."

A charming light played around Angelface's big blue eyes. "Elth you'll what?"

This was incredible! Here I was, standing with tea-stained feet, outside my very own modest suburban home, being intimidated by a little devil with a gap between his teeth.

I gathered together some kind of dignity. I'd tell them a thing or two, I thought, desperately trying to think up a thing or two to tell them. Then, astonishingly, Edward G. came to the rescue.

"Aw, c'mon," he muttered, "we'll play in the park." He gave me a lopsided smile. "Sorry, Missus, it's me little brother. Well, he can't help it, can he? He's got measles."

So that accounted for the rosiness of Angelface's countenance, and possibly even the venomous look he shot me as his elder relation dragged him away. I tossed the ball after them.

"Right! To the park — now!" I ordered, my morale almost restored. Edward G. caught the ball and waved a grubby hand at me in strangely adult acquiescence.

JUST as I had settled down once more for my elusive siesta the telephone rang. The petulant female voice at the other end asked me if I would go along immediately and remove *my* children from outside *her* café. The customers were beginning to get rather rattled about the perpetually bouncing ball which kept threatening them through the open window.

Already she had been forced to replace two cups of coffee and didn't I know that ball games weren't allowed in the street?

Is that what they call poetic justice? ■

"Would you have done more, if you hadn't married?" he countered.

"Nothing that mattered as much," she told him, meaning it.

He put down his empty coffee cup. "Ten years," he said softly, looking around. "Ten years ago since we came here and decided that we wanted more from life than marriage. Ten years since we said goodbye to each other, Beth."

He took both her hands in his.

"Brown hands," he said, and he smiled. "Brown from pushing prams and hanging out washing, and pulling weeds from the garden because your husband doesn't have time. Isn't that right?"

She flushed. "I like gardening," she replied. "And — all those things I do. They're worthwhile because they're for us, and for our children."

TAKING her by surprise, he drew her towards him until their lips met. It was a long kiss, long and warm and deep, and when his lips left hers, he kept her close to him.

"When did we change our minds, Beth?" he asked, his lips against her hair. "Was it that first holiday when I came home, and came to see you?"

She leaned against him, remembering. "And I thought you wouldn't be there till the next day, and I'd washed my hair, and I had on old jeans and no shoes."

She knew by his voice that he was smiling. "I'm sure it was then that I looked at you, and I thought — they can keep Harley Street, it's Beth I want."

He turned, and now his voice was anxious. "Beth — at the time I didn't really think of it, but — how much did you mind, giving up drama school and taking that office job so that we could be married?"

She didn't answer immediately. "Sometimes I minded," she said at last, slowly, honestly. "When I saw some of the other students, or when we went to plays — then I minded.

"But — those winter nights, Paul, when you were studying and we sat together at that awful little gas fire — I was happy, love, truly I was."

And then, a little uncertainly, because over the years they had got out of the habit of saying this sort of thing to each other, she went on . . .

"As I'm happy now, because we're together."

She put both the coffee cups back in the basket, glad to bend her head, glad to hide her suddenly flushed face. But all at once she had the certainty that this was the time to speak, for both of them. She sat back on her heels and looked at him.

"Sometimes recently," she began, feeling for the right words, "I've found myself thinking more and more of how it was for us ten years ago.

"We were so young, and — so much in love, and it seemed to me that we had lost the Paul and Beth who were like that. But — we hadn't lost them really, only lost sight of them.

"They're still there, and they're part of — of the Paul and the Beth we are now. Aren't they?" she asked him a little shakily.

"Of course they are," he told her. "Beth — I was afraid you would forget about today."

"And I was afraid you would," she replied. "And because I was afraid, I wouldn't let myself say or do anything to remind you. You — you had to remember by yourself, or it didn't mean anything."

And then, in case he misunderstood, she said quietly — "If you hadn't remembered, Paul, it wouldn't have made any difference. You're busy, and — we have so much, haven't we? The girls, and Steven, and — each other."

"And each other," he agreed. He hesitated, and then he looked at her, his grey eyes concerned. "Beth, you said you felt we'd lost the people we once were. I don't say to you often enough that I love you, that you mean everything to me."

"I don't say it to you, either," she returned, knowing this was true. "But we say it in other ways. You said it this morning, when you let me sleep because Steven was teething, when you brought tea for me."

"You say it too, love, every time you keep a meal hot for me when I'm late. But it wouldn't do us any harm to spell it out occasionally."

He stood up and pulled her to her feet. "I asked Johnny to take my lunchtime rounds at the hospital for me, but I'll have to get along there later. Can I take you out for lunch first?"

They began to walk down the hill, and halfway down, he looked down at her, and took her hand in his, as he had done all those years ago. And once again they ran down the hill, reaching the river flushed and breathless and laughing.

"We'll come here again, love, won't we?" he asked, all at once serious.

"Of course we will," she agreed. "And we'll bring the children."

He looked down at her. "Yes, we'll bring the children. but — sometimes, Beth, we'll come here on our own, just the two of us."

Just the two of us.

I'll remember this, she thought, as he kissed her, I'll remember it on those days when there seems to be no sunshine. I'll remember it, and I'll hold on to the truth of it.

For a moment, absurdly, she wished that she could take the perfection of the moment and wrap it up and put it away somewhere safe, to be taken out when she needed it.

Then she knew that she could do that — that she could wrap it up and keep it in her heart, and take it out when she needed it.

And she smiled with the sheer joy of this certainty as Paul took her hand in his and they turned to begin the journey home.

* **THE END** *

And Ring In The New

For them the New Year had always meant joy and celebration. Until this year — when there seemed nothing to look forward to . . .

A FEW dead leaves blown by the breeze made sad little sounds as they skimmed along the pavement.

Rita, looking from the window of the flat, thought how this used to be the time when she got out the cookery book, with Jimmy laughing at her, because she always planned her New Year buffet party long before Christmas. But the planning was fun, by the fire on a winter evening, getting ready for the highlight of the year.

This year was different. Jimmy had died in March, and the shock had changed Rita out of all recognition. She knew that until then she hadn't looked her thirty-eight years — hadn't looked much older than her seventeen-year-old daughter . . .

The thought of Frances and the quarrel they'd had came like a sudden pain. How could she be so selfish, Rita thought bitterly.

"But, Mummy, it's different this year . . ." Frances had protested, "I mean you don't *want* to have the buffet party, anyway . . ."

"I didn't anticipate seeing in the New Year alone," Rita had

Complete Story by AUDRIE MANLEY-TUCKER

retorted coldly, knowing she was handling the situation all wrong and not caring.

"Oh!" Frances sighed with exaggerated patience. "All right. I'll stay, and Anne's party was going to be such fun. Fancy dress and a treasure hunt . . ."

"And her father leaving you the house to yourselves, for the evening!"

"We're not kids," Frances had retorted with dignity. "And Anne's father trusts her."

Rita sighed and turned away from the window. She glanced at herself in the mirror, thinking how dreary she looked, and went downstairs to open the dress shop that she'd been running successfully since before Jimmy died.

Frances had already gone to the office, where she worked with Anne Gorham.

I don't much like Anne, Rita admitted honestly. And what on earth was Brian Gorham thinking of, letting her have a party on her own, at *her* age?

He had been in the town only a couple of years, replacing old Mr Stone as dental surgeon in the big house by the Common, but Rita had never met him.

She went into the shop, her thoughts far from the day's work ahead. New Year's Eve, she kept thinking miserably. Nan and Sheila and Stephen telling her to go ahead and have her party. Saying that she had to begin again somewhere . . . that they'd all come . . . and how it would do her good.

No, thought Rita stubbornly. That's no solution. And neither is keeping Frances as an unwilling partner to stave off a loneliness that never diminishes . . . it isn't the answer . . .

A MAN came into the shop just before closing time; fortyish, broad shouldered and compact, with nice brown eyes, and an air of being out of place in such surroundings.

"One of the jazzy new sweaters," he said earnestly, as though it was a well-learned lesson. "A greeny-blue shade; the fluffy kind — angora, isn't it? Size thirty-six . . . It's a birthday present, and she's been dropping hints . . ."

Rita's lips twitched slightly, but she said gravely, "We've been making a feature of them."

She spread a selection on the counter. He fingered the soft fabric, and she thought, absently, what nice hands he had.

"If it's the wrong size or colour, you can change it," she said.

He watched her wrap it; an assessing look. When he had gone, she frowned at herself in the mirror.

She was smooth and groomed because she had to be, her hair neat and styled, her skin pale and matt. But her eyes and mouth were bitter. Hard, she thought, suddenly — because of the wall around me since Jimmy's death.

The man was back next morning; a rueful smile on his face.

"It seems I didn't do so well." he told her wryly. "Thirty-four and long sleeves. Honestly, I'm awfully sorry."

"It's quite all right," she said crisply. "It often happens when men go shopping for their wives."

"My daughter," he told her, with a smile. "It's her birthday on Thursday."

Thursday, and Frances saying she'd get Anne the new LP she wanted, that six of them were going to the Chinese restaurant.

"She'll be eighteen, Mrs Harris," he told her.

"Yes." Her look was cool. So he'd known, all along, who she was, Rita thought.

"I like your daughter, Mrs Harris," he said. "She's teaching Anne to cook; she's bullied her into joining the Youth Club, and she's managing to strip away some of the shyness and awkwardness . . ."

Oh rubbish, Rita thought scornfully! Shy? Beneath those spiky lashes, the brittle manner? Still, maybe it was just possible . . .

"You don't like Anne," Brian Gorham said shrewdly.

He leant his elbows on the counter, looking at her in that penetrating way that made her feel too clearly scrutinised. "Now, why not?"

"My daughter's friends are her own affair," Rita retorted.

"True. I just wondered *why* you didn't. Maybe because Anne's

New Year party will mean that you're left alone, you felt bitter . . ."

"Is that what Frances told you?"

"No. But she told us about the fabulous buffet parties you gave, before her father died . . ."

Fabulous. Frances had seemed almost too resilient, bouncing back at life so easily, after her father's death. Perhaps it's easier when you're young, Rita thought painfully.

"Anne had an idea," he told her. "She thought it would be nice if you and I spent the evening together!"

Rita was furious. "How convenient! How ridiculous! Thank you, no!"

He nodded, unperturbed. "I knew you'd react that way. She was trying to be kind. I told her I wouldn't dream of it!"

She looked at him, her anger suddenly dissolving into resentment against him for his cool reprisal.

He saw her look, and said, smiling, "It wouldn't work, you know. We don't know one another. You don't like me, and I wouldn't want to spend the evening with a woman who was looking over her shoulder all the time.

"Oh, I know how you feel. It's four years since Becky, my wife, walked out on me. We'd been happy, but when she met this man, it seemed to turn her upside down. She left me, but she was coming back when she crashed the car. She died in hospital."

"I'm sorry," Rita said briefly. "It was worse for you, I suppose, knowing she was coming home . . . it all seems so senseless, like Jimmy dying suddenly, weeks after the promotion he'd waited years for . . . Nothing has made sense since then."

"New Year's Eve was special for us, too," he said reminiscently. "Ever since the first year we married. She was an ambitious cook, and she'd planned a special dish, duck, and a bottle of champagne.

"The cooking went all haywire, and I dropped the bottle and broke it; she cried, and then we laughed, and settled for macaroni cheese, which was all she could cook, and a bottle of wine we'd brought back from our Spanish honeymoon . . .

"Every year, after that, we saw New Year in, at home, with macaroni cheese and red wine. Sounds like something from a sentimental film, doesn't it?"

"What will you do, when Anne has her party?" she asked.

"Go to see a friend of mine. I'll leave about eleven, creep upstairs and read a good book in bed," he told her dryly. "Why don't you do the same?"

"So that Frances is free?" She shrugged. "Why not?"

He nodded. "You can't turn the clock back. Anne fusses after me like a mother hen. And it was thoughtful of her — if misguided — to think we might get acquainted over a dinner table on New Year's Eve. She thinks you're marvellous."

He was gone, and she felt irritated, disturbed by the truth of what he'd said.

Continued on page 54

THROUGH THE STORM TO OBERAMMERGAU

IN June 1970 I realised my great ambition!

You see, in the early, difficult years of the nineteen-thirties my friend and I, teenage schoolgirls at the time, had been inspired by a wonderful account of the famous Passion Play at Oberammergau. Its marvels had been so vividly described for us by our headmistress we declared that some day we would see it for ourselves.

We grew up and left school; the Second World War broke out, we both got married and had families. In a word, we were occupied with the cares of daily living.

But we never forgot our promise to each other to visit Oberammergau. And when, many years later, we heard more about its wonders from friends who went to see the 1960 Passion Play, we resolved that 1970 was to be our year.

Our children, we told each other, would be grown up. We ourselves would then be in our fifties, so we decided 1980 might be leaving things a little too late!

The Passion Play, of course, is only performed once every ten years.

So we began to save and plan and in 1968 we made our advance booking for June 1970.

As the time got nearer, I wondered how I should ever manage to afford this long-dreamed-of holiday. For I had a family of four children, all of whom had stayed on at school and then continued studying for professional qualifications. There had also been family health troubles which prevented my going out to work to supplement our income.

Then, right out of the blue, Fate stepped in and I received a small legacy just in time to pay the required advance holiday payment.

So Sunday, June 21, 1970, dawned, fair and sunny, a perfect day to set the pattern for a week of wonderful weather — a week perfect in every way.

The holiday we had chosen was to take us through eight different regions in Germany, with two nights in Oberammergau itself.

During that memorable week we passed through miles of beautiful countryside and stayed in luxurious hotels in beautiful cities. We lunched in the famous town of Heidelberg; we lunched on the shores of lovely Lake Constance.

We visited Donaueschingen, well-known as the source of the famous River Danube.

It was thrilling to see the fabulous River Rhine, flanked by vine-covered hillsides, its castles standing out against the skyline and the dark beetling face of the Lorelei Rock.

The Black Forest scenery, too, was

In 1990 thousands will make the "pilgrimage" to see the world-famous Passion Play at Oberammergau. Mrs Whittaker recalls the journey she made twenty years ago . . .

by
Mrs D.
WHITTAKER

Spectrum Colour Library

truly wonderful, as the sun poured down. Our coach climbed through the magnificent towering trees and, of course, we all had to take photographs whenever we stopped for a break!

THE highlight of the whole tour for us, naturally, was Oberammergau and the Passion Play. At last we were within a few hours' drive of our longed-for goal. We two, at least, were agog with excitement.

On Tuesday, June 23, we left the placid shores of Lake Constance and started the magnificent drive into the Alps, through Allgau, past Alpsee to Hingerlang. Now the scenery, began to look more threatening.

The mountains towered over us as the valley narrowed. Thunder cracked, and, as we stopped for a tea-break, a storm broke out and we had to make a dash for the coach.

There followed the most exciting and frightening part of the whole trip, a drive over the dangerous Oberjoch Pass through increasing darkness and storm.

Lightning lit up the sky almost constantly while thunder roared and rain lashed in torrential sheets down the windows of the coach. We swept down and down the narrow, winding roads towards Oberammergau.

But, at last, at about nine o'clock with the rain still pouring down and in pitch darkness, we had reached our destination.

Taxis had been organised to take us to our lodgings. For at that time visitors to the Oberammergau Passion Play were allotted rooms in the homes of the villagers.

We found ourselves in the home of a youngish German lady who spoke very little English. She took us to our room, which was very modern and comfortable.

Here, we found waiting for us one of our biggest thrills — set out on a small table were our tickets for the Play. Eagerly, we rushed over and picked them up. It was like finding gold at the rainbow's end!

After a late dinner at the Hotel Wolf, we were glad to tumble into

Continued from page 51

YOU don't have to spend New Year's Eve with me," she said to Frances that evening when she got back from work. "What sort of a fancy dress did you have in mind . . .?"

"Oh, Mum, thanks!" Frances was starry-eyed, flipping back the long, fair hair from her face, and adding innocently:

"Did Mr Gorham come in for Anne's birthday present?"

"He did. He also told me about the dinner-for-two idea. No need to look for amusements for me."

She saw the look on her daughter's face, and added more gently:

"This is the first year without your father . . . I suppose I'm touchy."

"I know!" Frances said miserably. "So I should stay and . . ."

"No. It's different for you. And I see you've left the cookery book very ostentatiously by my bed. But I couldn't, not this year, anyway. Besides, it's foolish to look back."

On Mondays, Rita always closed the shop all day. The following Monday, she whisked through her housework, and put on a thick, scarf-collared tweed coat.

There was a café on the edge of town, famous for cream teas, and she didn't have to worry about her figure . . .

It was less than four weeks to Christmas, and she didn't feel like making any effort at all. Only for Frances' sake, she thought. She remembered Jimmy hanging up the football socks he hadn't used since he was at school, singing carols outside the bedroom door on Christmas morning, and she suddenly felt lonelier and more desolate than she had since his death.

As she stepped from the café, seeing the street through a blur of tears, Brian Gorham's car pulled up at the kerb.

Continued from previous page

bed, weary but so happy.

Next morning, we were up very early, for we had to be in our seats at the theatre at 8.15 a.m. So it was an early breakfast for everyone!

Luckily, the famous open-air theatre was only a short distance away. When we arrived, we found our seats were in a wonderful position, quite central and near enough to the front. They were far better than we had ever dared to expect.

We were just too excited for words. The theatre was packed and everyone seemed friendly. Soon we were chatting away to people from all over the world.

Then, finally, the play began and the hush that fell on that great crowd was almost unbelievable. There was not a sound from them until the interval at twelve noon. Everyone seemed gripped by the wonderful story of Jesus' last week on earth, which was being brought so vividly to life before our eyes.

After a lunch interval of two hours the audience were back in their seats to witness more drama of the highest quality.

The Crucifixion scene was poignantly real. And a terrific, but very brief thunderstorm during Peter's

"If you're going back to the shop," he said casually, "then I'm going your way."

He glanced at her face, and said, "You look as if you're in for a bout of flu."

She shook her head, not caring enough to pretend. "I was looking back. Stupid, you'd call it, remembering the silly things Jimmy and I did at Christmas."

"I wouldn't say stupid," he said gently. "Inevitable, but foolish. In time, you only look back occasionally, I think. Becky and I had wonderful times at Christmas."

Deliberately, she changed the conversation.

"No patients this afternoon?"

"Two late afternoon ones. Monday is my quiet day. My daughter told me the other day that it was a terribly unromantic profession — pulling teeth, filling teeth, making dentures. She said dental surgeons were like mothers-in-law, only good for TV jokes!"

For the first time, she laughed with him.

Then she said, "I hated going to the dentist. Jimmy knew that, so every time I had an appointment he arranged for a bunch of flowers to be delivered at the same time from the local florists' — just to make sure I'd collect them! It was the sweetest thing anyone ever did for me!"

"You were lucky," he said quietly. "Remember that. Anne and Frances have been getting together — I thought I should warn you. They think we need help, you to face the New Year, me to be jolted out of my comfortable rut. The latest idea is that we should go to *their* party."

"Oh no!" Rita said firmly. "I'd feel like a fish out of water."

She was silent until they reached the flat. She thanked him and scurried indoors, glad to be out of the cold wind. She felt exhausted,

Continued on page 58

---

denial of Jesus rolled in from the surrounding mountains. As he flung himself down in remorse, the rain poured down, as if to enhance the awe-inspiring grandeur of the whole scene. Then, during the Resurrection scene the sun burst out and shone in the most spectacular way. It was all the more moving because it was not organised by man, but an act of God Himself.

PEOPLE in the village told us that something similar had occurred at every performance up to that date. And the Play had already been running about six weeks!

After the heights and depths of that great Passion Play, which had in every way exceeded our expectations, what more is there to say?

All the rest, inevitably, was something of an anti-climax. It was a wonderful day, an unforgettable experience, and certainly one of the most memorable of my life.

Nevertheless, the sun was shining again and we had many more beautiful places to see before our return home.

And, just to remind me that it all really happened, I still treasure that precious ticket for the Play and carry it with me everywhere, safe inside my notecase, a constant reminder of my holiday of a lifetime. ■

A BADGER

WHEN friends brought the young badger to me I wasn't quite sure if he was sleeping or dead. They'd found him in the woods after a dog had attacked him and now he was looking very sorry for himself.

I held him in my arms until I felt his body get a bit warmer. After a while he opened one eye and gave me a long look. It was the beginning of our friendship.

Of course, he had to have something to eat. Would he like a dish of warm milk?

I put it in front of him. He sniffed at it, got it in his nose and started to sneeze. Well, he probably was not yet able to drink from a saucer and I tried to feed him with a baby bottle. But he just didn't take to it.

In the end I tried an eyedropper, opening his mouth and spraying the milk in. Quite a bit ran out of the other side of his mouth, but at least he got something in his stomach.

Life soon became a matter of routine. Bonnie, as I called the little badger, was fed every three hours with half a cup of warm milk with baby cereal mixed in. Later on I increased the amount to a full cup or more at a time.

It seemed to suit him. He grew bigger and fatter. After three weeks he started to eat from a saucer and I began to give him some fine minced meat (sometimes cooked, sometimes raw).

When he was small, Bonnie slept in a box in the living-room. But when he got bigger he was locked in the kitchen during the night.

But he very soon learned to open cupboards and was banished to spend the night in a large cage in the garden.

During the day he was free and could go wherever he wanted, but as this was his real sleeping time, he mostly settled down to a snooze under my bed. When he woke up in the evening it was playtime for him, and as he got older and stronger, he turned everything upside down and nothing was safe from him any more.

When it was dark, I took him out into the garden. He never went on his own and only felt safe when I was with him. As soon as I walked back to the house Bonnie came bounding after me.

IN the house he found lots of things to amuse him. Shoes would disappear and he hid small odds and ends in them as well.

He used to swing on towels hung up on the back of the door and, if they fell down, he "killed" them at once. When they were quite "dead" he got bored and left them lying on the floor.

The telephone was fascinating for the little badger. Whenever he heard it ringing he would settle down in front of it. He knew somebody would come soon to answer the phone and would probably sit on the stairs.

Bonnie would go one step higher, stand on his hind legs and put his front legs around the neck of the person talking. Did he want to hear what was going on? Or was he just pleased to find someone to play with?

When he was let out of his cage in the morning, he had his breakfast and climbed upstairs. After he had a look through all the cupboards, he took out various odds and ends — things he liked most — and went under my bed. He carefully arranged them before he went to sleep.

One morning he discovered a box of paper handkerchiefs in a cupboard. He must have thought them particularly beautiful, be-

BY MRS HEDE STEWART

ABOUT THE HOUSE

cause he arranged them artistically over the whole house.

It took us some time to find them all again and we decided we might as well make him a present of them and put them in his sleeping box. They made a wonderful soft bed for him.

But one morning he was in a particularly bad mood. He didn't eat a bit of his breakfast and went straightaway upstairs.

A few minutes later I heard what sounded like a small thunderstorm from up there and when I went to see what was going on, I found him lying on my bed. That was a bit much, I thought, and pushed him off.

Finding himself under the bed again, he discovered that he couldn't sleep without his bits and pieces and he went on an exploring trip.

As my parents were staying with us at the time, he decided to pay them a visit. After a while there came a rustling noise and Bonnie appeared with my father's trousers behind him!

He pulled them under the bed and went to sleep at once. But Father was not very amused when he couldn't find his trousers when he got up!

WHEN Bonnie was nearly five months old we had to make a decision where it was best to release him. After all, he was a wild animal and we wanted him to be free.

One day we were told of a couple, living nearly three hundred miles away, who had prepared tame badgers for the wild before.

They owned a lonely cottage surrounded by woods, but the best thing of all was an artificial badger sett in their garden and a trap-door for badgers in the garden wall. Bonnie would slowly lose his tameness there and learn to look after himself.

So the day came when we had to say "Goodbye."

Bonnie was very excited. He knew there was something going on. When I held him in my arms for the last time, he stuck his nose in my ear and put his paws in my hair.

It was very difficult to let him go. His new home was a long way away. I would never see him again.

I put him into his transport cage. He bit and tried with all his strength to get out.

Continued overleaf

Continued from page 55
and thought longingly of bed. But it was almost their busiest time, and tomorrow the new assistant was coming for the Christmas season.

YOU look awful," Frances said critically, when she came home. "Go to bed."

Rita obeyed meekly. Frances brought her a beautifully-laid supper tray. Later on, she heard Anne arrive and the two of them were giggling in the kitchen.

She drifted into sleep and, when she woke, Anne was coming into the room, nervous, smiling uncertainly.

"Orange snow," she said. "Frances showed me how to make it. I hope you'll soon be better."

Under all that make-up, the manners of a polite, thoughtful child, Rita thought. Children grew up, and Anne was doing most of hers without any feminine guidance. It couldn't be easy.

She managed a smile.

"It looks delicious," she said.

Rita insisted on opening the shop next day; the new assistant was sensible, mid-thirtyish.

Together, they dressed the window with pretty gimmicks and costume jewellery. They hung silver bells on red ribbons, and bunched frosted holly high in a corner of the window. Rita climbed out of the window, feeling stiff and cold.

She stayed on her feet for a week. At the end of that time, she was too ill to care whether it was Christmas or high summer. She lay between sheets that felt as though they were red-hot and her head a football being kicked up and down a field . . . it hurt to breathe.

She was vaguely aware that Frances or Anne brought her things that were blessedly cold to drink . . .

IT was only a few days to Christmas when she sat up, feeling hungry, and weak. The roofs of the shops opposite were sugared

Continued from previous page

I tried to talk to my little badger, but he couldn't understand why I had betrayed him in this way. However, when we put a blanket over the cage he became quieter and settled down.

Soon he would be in his new home. It was the last time he was caged, and we hoped that he would have a good life as a wild badger.

When the car disappeared into the next road, we went back into the house. It was very quiet and empty without Bonnie.

Four months later, we learned Bonnie was independent. He had dug himself a sett in the woods, kept away from people and was completely self-supporting.

But occasionally, in the mud near the cottage, we still see the unmistakable mark of a badger's footprints. So perhaps our Bonnie thinks of us from time to time. I hope so. ■

with frost; a row of cards stood on the mantelpiece, and there were grapes beside her bed.

"Thank heavens!" Frances said fervently. "Dr Johns will be pleased!"

"The shop!" Rita said, dismayed.

"Mrs Wilson is coping beautifully. Anne and I took some time off — a solicitor's office is always quiet, this time of year and Mr Parkes didn't mind us taking leave when I said you were ill.

"We helped her out. It was fun. I've got in most of the stuff we need for Christmas, and Anne's father sent the grapes."

Frances sounded casually unconcerned, as though she had taken it all in her stride as a matter of course and sudden pride made Rita want to weep. Frances, she thought, was Jimmy's best-ever gift to her.

It was Christmas Eve before she went down to the shop. It was the middle of the afternoon, and they were busy. Anne and Frances and Mrs Wilson. They were coping so effortlessly that she felt unnecessary.

"I don't know what I'd have done without you," she told them, including Anne in the words.

Anne flushed, looking pleased.

"I'm cooking Christmas dinner tomorrow," she said. "First time. Last year and the year before we went to a hotel. We thought it was time we had a proper at-home Christmas."

Upstairs, in the flat that evening. Rita watched Frances threading tinsel through the branches of the small tree.

"It's going to be dull for you," she fretted.

Frances looked surprised. "Christmas? No, that's a family get-together, isn't it? Anne and I are going to compare notes, Boxing Day, on how we cooked the turkey! By the way, I told you about the party at the club on Boxing Night, didn't I?"

Her fingers were clumsy, and she turned her head away. "Richard is club leader, and he specially asked me to help: and you remember Donald Simon — he came here once? He's keen on Anne, I think.

And she likes him. Will you hate being alone on Boxing Night?"

"No," said Rita firmly. "Nor on New Year's Eve!"

It wasn't true, but she didn't regret the lie. She wondered what Brian Gorham was doing at Christmas. She'd telephoned him and thanked him for the grapes, and he had been pleasantly friendly, pleased that she was getting better.

He sent her a Christmas present, a potted plant with an exotic name. Anne said jubilantly that the dinner had been a success, it had been just the two of them, but she hadn't minded that. It had been fun . . .

She went off on Boxing Night with stars in her eyes, and wearing a becoming new dress. She's pretty, Rita thought; not with Frances' leggy grace that will turn to elegance, but with a warmth about her . . .

Continued on page 62

LOUIE MY WARTIME BUDDY

BY MR MULLINGTON

IT was during the war that I first met and adopted my friend Louie. At the time I was in the Army, a wireless operator attached to a battalion of infantry, and in Italy.

Our convoy had just pulled into a farm which had been overtaken by the war and was suffering from the effects.

Some of the farm animals had been killed and I remembered a huge white ox with a shrapnel wound in its thigh, standing patiently in the farmyard. Someone had clumsily bandaged the wound with a field dressing, no doubt with the object of stopping the bleeding.

I have always felt a great regard for animals and was impressed by this act of kindness.

While wandering around the farm I discovered a hutch occupied by four or five young rabbits. The one that took my eye was unquestionably the ugliest and the most comical specimen I had ever seen.

A rather long gaunt face that possessed a distinct belligerent expression was topped by the left ear standing stiff and erect in the orthodox rabbit fashion, while the right one hung limply down like when you first start skinning a banana!

Although he accepted me as his friend, he was always ready to prove his independence, and I felt sure he never really got over the insult of my calling him Louie.

At the particular time it appeared to me that our common enemy — I say common enemy because I felt sure that Louie was on our side although he came of Italian stock — was steadily retreating and we, for our part, leisurely advancing.

So I had time to be with Louie during his early infancy, and I gave him the opportunity to understand a little of the English language.

He grew and adapted himself to army life very quickly. And I made him a small hutch, which he himself decided to use only when travelling.

ON arrival at the places we were destined to make camp, my first obligation was to remove Louie's hutch from my wireless truck, place it on the ground and open the door.

Louie would be out in a flash and, with nose twitching, he would tilt back his head, causing the limp ear to swing like a pendulum. He'd make several jumps around the hutch and then take off like he had gone berserk.

Each time this happened someone was bound to say, "That's it, he's gone this time, you've seen the last of him."

But Louie was no deserter and back he would come, even though on occasions he left it till the last moment — like the time when we stayed at a deserted farm . . .

This particular location was not altogether a peaceful one, owing to spasmodic bursts of mortar fire from the Germans. So I decided against my usual practice of giving Louie his freedom and instead established him in an empty pig-sty and collected his food myself.

I was actually doing this when I heard for the first time the *Nebelwerfer* — the dreaded German mortar — explode. I don't think I've ever heard a more soul-destroying row in all my life and I lost no time in getting back inside the farmhouse.

When the time came for us to move on, I went to collect Louie from the sty but found to my annoyance that

someone had removed the brick blocking the drain off from the sty enclosure. Louie had gone!

I put down his hutch and despondently made my way to my truck, parked a good half mile away alongside the rest of the section's vehicles. It was only then I saw him — Louie... sitting calmly washing his face, getting ready to move out with us. You may think it was a coincidence, but it wasn't the only time Louie decided to turn up at moving-out time.

At the back of my mind I hoped that, come the end of the war, I'd somehow get Louie back home with me. What a sensation this little fellow would cause!

To me Louie was unique, and I was convinced that everyone back home would think so, too. However, like so many anticipated and looked-for pleasures, this was doomed to disappointment.

Returning to my section one night after a hectic spell of action, I was looking forward to seeing that ugly mug grinning a welcome. But there was no Louie and I sensed he'd gone for ever this time.

I stood in the growing darkness looking down at the little hutch he'd escaped from. Then I raised my eyes to the nearby fields and said softly, "Goodbye, Louie, you take care, you hear."

Now, looking back, I like to think that, having got out, Louie went to look for me and in doing so found happiness on the way. I hope so. I'll never forget that ugly — but wonderful little fellow. ■

Continued from page 59

Brian Gorham might telephone on Boxing Night, she thought. But he didn't, and she felt unjustifiably hurt. At half-past ten, she lifted the receiver, and when he answered, she thanked him for his plant.

"Glad you liked it," he said. "Glad you're better, too. How was Christmas?"

"Better than I expected," she admitted truthfully.

"Good." He might have been a doctor with a new prescription. "I'll send you a book to read in bed on New Year's Eve. There's a new one out by an author that Frankie says is a favourite of yours . . ."

"Thanks," she said coldly. "I won't need it."

"So you're going to the kids' party after all?"

"No!" she retorted, annoyed.

"So it's the dinner for two, then . . .?"

"*You* turned that down!" she retorted, furious with him. "Saying you wouldn't dream of it, that it wouldn't work because we don't know one another, and you didn't want to spend an evening with a woman who looked over her shoulder all the time!"

"So you remembered all that?" he said softly. "Well, we've got better acquainted since then, haven't we?"

"I don't need anyone to feel sorry for me," she told him. And thought, as she replaced the receiver, that the remark had a teenage flavour making her seem silly and petulant.

SHE hated the days between Christmas and New Year, the frayed end of the old year, she thought.

And this time, none of the preparations, the excitement, the looking-forward to the party that began at eight, and never ended until one o'clock, with Jimmy making tea for everyone, and people asking her how did she do it, saying her ideas for a buffet table were so original she ought to sell them . . .

New Year's Eve will be worse than Christmas, she thought; it was too big an effort to try and fight the misery she felt. Frances was subdued, as though she felt she had no right to be making plans for a wonderful evening.

"Enjoy it, darling." Rita said determinedly. At least, she thought thankfully, I have come this far; I understand Frances.

"Are Richard and Donald going to be there?" she asked.

"Of course." Frances pirouetted in front of the mirror, and suddenly she was fumbling for words.

"It seems so silly . . . Anne's father is going out to a meal all on his own."

"I expect he prefers it that way," Rita said casually.

The flat seemed intolerably empty after Frances' departure; the memories crowded back, jostling for elbow room. Twenty people, the big doors folded back, the laughter, the door bell ringing . . .

The door bell rang — once. She almost knocked over a lamp,

getting up from her chair. She was wearing slacks and a bright silk shirt, and her hair was tousled.

Brian Gorham was standing on the doorstep; it was the first time she had seen him since the day he had given her a lift.

"You'll need something warmer than that," he said, eyeing her shirt.

"What do you mean?" She felt at a loss, all hands and feet, as she stood aside for him to come in. It was because she'd been ill, she told herself. She'd never lacked poise, Jimmy had once said, not even in the most difficult situation.

"You're looking fine," he told her approvingly. He smiled. "What do I mean? Well, I have a fancy to see the New Year in from Beacon Hill.

"I've been up there once or twice, after dark. Glorious views, all the lights of town below. To be up above the world, toast the New Year in — yes, that would be a good beginning. You'd have to wrap up warmly, and stay in the car. Still, you might enjoy it."

"Frances said you were going out to dinner on your own," she stammered.

"Was I?" He looked at her with wicked, little-boy innocence. "Could be I'd changed my mind. The local delicatessen made up a wonderful hamper for me. I've filled a flask with hot coffee, and I've got a bottle of wine."

"Spanish wine?" she said.

"No," he told her, not pretending to understand. "Not the kind that goes with macaroni cheese because the duck was burnt and the champagne spilled. That wine belongs to yesterday."

"Like my buffet parties," she said, with a rueful smile that came to the edge of tears.

"Yes. You should only look back to remember with happiness, to smile, not to be sad. You were furious with me because I didn't want to have dinner with you. But at least being angry woke you up just a little, didn't it?"

She looked at him. Just a little, she thought. Well, *more* than that. She'd had time to think since the day he first walked into the shop.

"So," said Brian Gorham, "how do you like the idea of seeing the New Year in from the top of Beacon Hill? And drinking a toast to a better year than the one you've just had?"

Impulsively, she put out a hand.

"I'd like it very much!" she told him.

He took her fingers in his, and squeezed them gently.

His hand felt warm, Rita thought, and some of the warmth spread through to the small, cold place at the centre of her, and she began to feel excited, as though the evening could have some special meaning, hidden still, but there, waiting . . .

*** THE END ***

Once Upon A Time

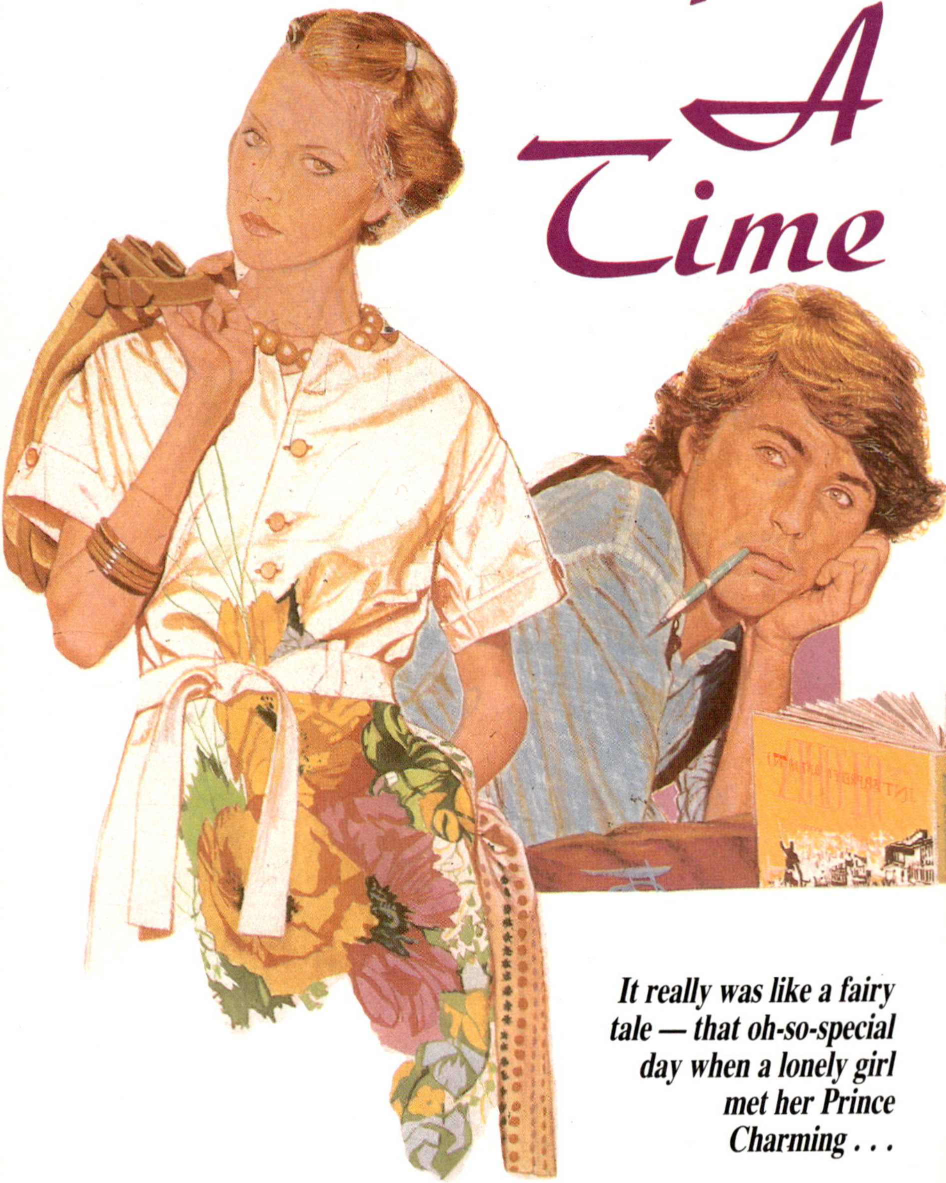

It really was like a fairy tale — that oh-so-special day when a lonely girl met her Prince Charming . . .

Complete Story By ELIZABETH ASHCROFT

I SIT here in my small studio flat high above London's roof-tops, looking down at the evening paper.

It's open at the radio and TV page, and my gaze is riveted to a paragraph at the head of the page. I stare out over the shining wet roof-tops, and remember the jungly green day.

I was fifteen and playing truant . . .

I'd never done it before, and already, walking hurriedly up the short-cut to the river and woods, I was scared. Scared of my aunt and uncle, if they found out, scared of what they would say at school.

If Miss Lewis, my favourite teacher, discovered I'd played truant, I thought miserably, she'd never speak to me again. I remembered her in the classroom the previous afternoon.

"If you work hard, Jennifer, you'll get a place at university. Your aunt would be so pleased. And so would I."

The trouble was, I hated the thought of university. I was a solitary person, the unknown shadowy figures of the future whom I would have to meet filled me with awe.

How was I ever going to manage to become an adult, I wondered, catching my beret on an overhanging twig. Suddenly I wished, much too late, that I'd never dreamed of playing truant, today of all days.

It was my birthday. And that morning, looking at Aunt Jessie, thin and grey, smiling palely at me over the book token she'd given me, and Uncle Thomas, his glasses slipped down his nose and his cardigan already spotted with toast crumbs, I suddenly hated them both. They'd never given me anything but dutiful affection.

True, they'd taken me in three years before, after my parents had been killed in a plane crash on a package holiday. But I'd never really felt welcome in their neat little bungalow.

Aunt Jessie had made me her life's work. She was childless, through choice, I imagined, since Uncle Thomas needed as much mothering as she could supply. She made such an effort of looking after me I was continually on edge.

She nagged me about coats and boots in the winter, and worried about the heat and sunstroke in the summer. I grew so self-contained it hurt — I could never talk to her about private, secret things, as I'd done with my mother . . .

And today I'd finally rebelled.

It was early summer, and one of those mornings when I couldn't bear to be indoors. Suddenly, at the door of the bungalow, I'd known I wouldn't go to school.

"Don't be late, Jennifer," Aunt Jessie said, tucking my scarf in the neck of my brown mac. I fidgeted helplessly.

"All right," I muttered, and that was when I felt the sun warm on my back, and smelled the crisp tang of a late frost.

I dreaded the stuffy over-heated classrooms at the grammar school . . .

I hated that school, too. In fact, I seemed to hate everything and everyone — except Miss Lewis.

So I waved to Aunt Jessie and walked slowly down the street to the bus stop. But at the end of the road, I turned abruptly into the lane.

It ran all the way up behind our road of bungalows, and was used as a dumping ground for old broken bottles; for walking the dogs; and by courting teenagers whom I both envied and hated at the same time.

I glanced at my watch. It was nine o'clock, so Assembly had just begun. Right now Pru, the nearest to a best friend I had, would be wondering what had happened to me.

I hesitated. It still wasn't too late. I could run all the way, say I'd overslept, join them at Biology. No-one would ever know how near to truancy I'd been.

Then I remembered the surprise on the girls' faces who'd been biking to school, as they saw me striding determinedly in the opposite direction. It was too late . . .

I trudged up the lane, disregarding the birds darting across the path, the excited twittering as a blackbird dropped a piece of bread almost at my feet. Already I was hungry, and I felt in my satchel. There was a bar of chocolate and a currant bun for morning break, and that was all.

I came to the top of the path, looking across into the woods. There was nowhere else I could go. If I went to the town someone would be sure to see me.

I ran quickly across the road, and into the woods, and panic left me. There was no sound, save that of my feet scrunching along in the old leaves, and suddenly, I felt a sense of overwhelming freedom.

EVERYTHING was fresh, green smelling, still with a hint of frost in the air. Looking round delightedly, I saw a huge intricate spider's web just in front of me, tipped with frost, so it looked like one of Aunt Jessie's best lace table mats.

"Hi," a voice said close behind me.

I jumped, staring wide-eyed at the boy leaning nonchalantly against a tree trunk.

He was watching me with an odd expression, surprise and curiosity mingled, and his hair was short and fairish. He was wearing jeans and a sweater.

"Hello," I stammered. He grinned widely, showing very white teeth.

"Playing truant?" he asked carelessly, and my face went hot.

"How did you know?"

"You look scared," he said. "The way I did when I first stayed off. Here, come and sit on this log."

He patted a log beside him and brushed it carefully, still grinning. "Mustn't get your nice coat all dirty. What would Mum say when you got home?"

I didn't like him. He was the sort of boy I'd always avoided.

"I haven't got a mother," I said bleakly. To my utter horror my eyes filled with tears, and he was a blurred misty figure against the sunlight slanting through the bare tree trunks.

He straightened. "Neither have I. Or a father."

"Nor me," I said. "They were killed in a plane crash."

"Nothing so exciting for mine," he said caustically, sitting on the log. "My dad walked out. My mum got pneumonia. I live with my older sister, and she can't stand the sight of me."

I felt a sudden surge of pity. He did look neglected. A long strand of cotton hung from the front pocket of his jeans, and his shoes were shabby. At least Aunt Jessie and Uncle Thomas cared for me, in an offhand, not-liking-to-show-it way.

"What made you skip school today?" he asked abruptly.

I went over to him and sat down on the hard knobbly tree trunk. I

Operation "Cover-Up"

YOU get an hour's warning. Friends you haven't seen for some time are coming to see you.

Of course, it's the day you've been doing a huge washing, or cleaned out the attic, or been in town all morning and let the housework go to hang! It always is.

Still, you have that precious hour in which to do a hectic rush job of keeping up appearances.

The thing is, what do you do with that hour?

That was the question that came up recently when a few of us (working wives) had met for a cup of tea and a chat.

Most of us plumped for a frantic dash round with vacuum and duster, but only in the rooms our visitors would be likely to see.

Other's favoured a cover-up job — throwing all the bits and pieces lying around out of sight and hoping for the best.

So far, only one of the crowd had said nothing and inevitably we all turned to her to ask which of the two "methods" she used.

"Neither," she said with a smile. "All I do is go out into the garden and pick a huge bunch of flowers. I then arrange it in a most prominent place.

"You'd be amazed at what you can get away with that way."

I must admit I liked her method best. I hadn't thought of creating a diversion.

And what nicer diversion than the eye-catching beauty of a bowl of flowers?

I wonder what method you use?

stared down at my functional knee socks and wished for the twentieth time Aunt Jessie would let me buy tights, like Pru wore to school.

"It's my birthday," I said. "And nobody seemed to care about it. I just — suddenly — wanted to get away from them all. That's all."

"Happy birthday," he said.

★ ★ ★ ★

I looked round the little clearing. A few trees had fallen down and lay with roots sticking pathetically up through the long grass. There were fir trees rustling high above, and underfoot, layer upon layer of pine needles. They were like the softest carpet in the world, I thought, with sudden wonder.

I wished abruptly I'd my sketching pad in my satchel, and a pencil.

"Why did you come?" I asked with sudden curiosity.

"Just wanted to think. To get away from everyone, like you. I can't stand school. They spend all their time trying to make me do woodwork, or geography, or play football. That's no use to me."

He spoke with a sort of scorn. I was envious, wishing I too could feel scorn instead of awe and fear.

"Why? What do you want to do?"

He stared at me as though I were slow-witted. "Write, of course."

He spoke with an odd sort of purpose, and I felt with a strange certainty that if he wanted to write he would. He was about a year older than me, but seemed almost a man, with an air of authority about him.

"Do you come here a lot, then? To think out stories, and things?" I'd never met a writer before, and I was awed.

"Yes. I do my writing here. It's the only place I can get any peace. My sister's kids are all over me at home." He gestured downwards and I saw he had an exercise book on the ground beside him, and two pencils sat neatly side by side on the grey cover.

"It's all I ever wanted to do," he said. "What do you want to do when you leave school?"

I hesitated. I'd not told anyone of my longing to be an artist. Art classes were all I could think of, all I looked forward to at school. It was an escape, a running away from life, an adventure into make-believe that filled me with delight and longing.

I would stare at the students coming out of the local art school with an envious longing.

"I want to be an artist," I said hesitantly, and somehow, actually speaking, telling someone about it, made it more real. I sensed his eyes on me.

"You good at it, then?"

"Not bad," I said airily. Then I scuffed despondently in the pine needles. "My aunt wants me to go to university, though. She wants me to be a teacher."

"But you just want to paint? Live in a room and turn out a masterpiece a week?"

He was so near to my dream I glanced at him swiftly, and our eyes met.

His eyes were dark blue, with enormously long lashes, and I felt suddenly uncomfortable. I'd never met anyone like him before, so direct and compelling, and suddenly I was afraid.

"That's part of my future, too," he said lazily. "Just to be on my own, and write."

"Could you make enough money at it?" I asked naïvely, and he grinned.

"Shan't know until I try. Hey, what's your name?"

"Jennifer Adams," I replied uncertainly.

"I'm Joe. Here, let's go and look at the river. You can get to it down this path here. It would be drier sitting down there."

I hesitated.

"Well?" he asked impatiently. "You coming or not?"

Aunt Jessie was at the back of my mind, with her anxious roundabout warnings of strange men, never speaking to strangers. But I was strong, I thought. I could look after myself. He seemed to sense my thoughts.

"I won't hurt you!" he exclaimed scornfully. "You flatter yourself!"

He was rude, and common, I thought crossly. But I plunged down after him, along the sloping, winding path. Suddenly I didn't want to be alone, here in the woods. They were too big, and there were odd little rustling noises. I kept very close behind him, almost touching him, and when he stopped abruptly I cannoned into him.

"Look!" he hissed. "Squirrels!"

He pointed, and up in the fir trees, chasing each other up and down the branches, tails high in the air, were three squirrels.

"Oh, they're lovely!"

He turned to me. "Never seen them before?"

I shook my head.

"You've a lot more to see, then. Come on. I'll show you a badger's sett."

THAT was the beginning of the jungly green day, as I always thought of it afterwards. He led me cautiously to the sett, and told me he'd actually seen the badgers at night, dancing in the moonlight.

"Mum badger and all the little badgers," he said softly.

"I'd love to see them," I breathed.

He glanced at me. "You can come one night, if you like," he said. But we both knew I never would. I could never get away from Aunt Jessie, for one thing. For another, I was too scared.

We half sat, half squatted, on the loamy dark earth, and the smell of spring was all around — a green, earthy, fresh smell.

"It's a sort of jungly green smell," I said involuntarily, and he stared at me in surprise.

Continued on page 73

HAVE you ever been to a jumble sale? Not those genteel functions which are usually opened with full ceremony by an inaudible lady in a large hat.

On such occasions, one can buy a "nice" potted plant for Aunt Maud from stalls kept by "nice" ladies in nylon overalls. These affairs are the aristocrats of the jumble sale world.

Now the real thing is quite different!

For a start there's no opening ceremony — the doors open and that's it.

It's a rough, tough, free-for-all where the stallholders are brawny individuals chosen for stamina rather than sales-ability and the best man, or more frequently woman, wins.

At one period in his career, my eldest son had a passion for collecting old 78 r.p.m. records. Jumble sales were a great source and he would travel for miles just to sort through a selection of cracked discs.

"You must come, Mum," I remember him saying once. "They've got some terrific things there. I've got my own money — and you might even get something for Dad's birthday there!"

I shuddered to imagine my husband's reactions to a present from such a source. But weakly protesting, I eventually gave in.

Not being well versed in the rules of the game, I decked myself out in my best coat, high-heeled shoes and gloves, not realising that boots and denims would have filled the bill much better.

Under my eldest's guidance we caught the bus to a tough neighbourhood which seemed to have its fists permanently at the ready.

Nevertheless, the local inhabitants that we met greeted us amiably, and several, who had obviously met my eldest before, hailed him as an old friend.

"Mrs Thomson's Marlene's sent a lot down," he was told by one fellow regular.

"Look for old Joe Green. He's saving you some," another informed him confidentially.

I looked at my eldest with some respect. He was obviously "well-in" and had cornered the market in this particular area.

We stood around shuffling our feet, until a slight forward movement showed that someone had opened the doors farther

"YOU CAN'T HAV

You can help your garden fet
the hurly-burly, roug

By Mrs M. LANGDON

down the road. Our momentum increased until we, too, were paying at the door for the privilege of being hurtled down a flight of bare wooden stairs into the hall beyond.

THE noise hit me first — a battering, ear-shattering roar — which went on and on without pause. Hundreds of voices plus the steady tramp and shuffle of hundreds of feet on the bare boards made an indescribable din.

I glanced at my eldest to see his reaction but he was already plunging head-first into this seething mass of humanity.

My highly-polished shoes began to look as though they'd been in a rugby scrum and after receiving several excruciating kicks on the ankle I headed into the fray in the same grim spirit as everyone else.

Fortunately, my eldest knew his way around as we soon halted at a large trestle table running the width of the hall where the choicer items of the sale were on display.

An elderly man with a cloth cap and a drooping white moustache — I assume this was "old Joe Green" — seemed to be the referee at this end of the hall.

"Hello, me old mate!" he

THOSE, I'M WEARING THEM!"

d your summer fayres, says Mrs M. Langdon. Give me d-tumble of a good old jumble sale any time!

greeted my son boisterously. "I see you've brought your mum this time. Pleased to meet you." He beamed at me, enveloping us both in his friendly hospitality.

My eldest beamed back and under Joe's instructions fought his way to the end of the stall, where the precious pile of "Marlene's" records was lying.

While my son was sifting through them, I turned to have a good look at what was going on around me.

Large, solidly-built trestles had been formed into a circle and all the coats, skirts, trousers and what-have-you had simply been piled in mad confusion on this hastily-provided counter space.

The crowd was at least six deep round this centre-stand, a cheerful, determined mass which pushed, jostled and kicked in an attempt to reach the front row.

Everyone shouted, everyone pushed, and I watched and listened, fascinated, until a tug at my coat indicated that my eldest had taken his pick and was ready to make for home.

"Could you carry them for me for a minute, Mum?" he pleaded. "There's something else I want."

MEEKLY I took charge of about a dozen records, and arranged to meet him outside. Edging round the scrum, I headed for the door and the wonderful smell of fresh air.

I leaned pallidly against the wall and took stock of myself. My shoes were a disgrace, my tights were full of holes and the top button of my coat was hanging dejectedly by a single thread. My already low spirits sank a few degrees further as my eldest emerged from the bargain basement carrying something which was just, but only just recognisable as a vacuum-cleaner.

"Look, Mum! I got this for you!" he announced with a beaming smile. "And it only cost fifty pence!

"Thank you, dear. That was kind of you," I murmured, seeing already in my mind's eye all the cogs and screws and intestines of the thing strewn over his bedroom floor.

But, for once, my pessimism was unjustified.

Back home, as I kicked off my shoes and wriggled the circulation back into my toes, surrounded by the peace and warmth of my own kitchen, my son disappeared upstairs.

I had only just sipped my way through one cup of tea when the unmistakable drone of a vacuum-cleaner began to rattle the tea-cups.

A moment or two later, my eldest charged into the kitchen with the sweeper working full blast, only just missing the cat's tail and picking up every movable object in its path.

"It works, Mum! I told you!" he crowed, as the contraption began to eat up the edges of the rug. My delight was only equalled by my surprise. Between us, we did every carpet downstairs and then returned to the kitchen, where we relaxed with more tea.

My son's face took on a thoughtful expression. "That was a good bargain, Mum," he reflected.

I agreed enthusiastically.

Pensively reaching for his coat and making for the door, he remarked as if to no-one in particular:

"I wonder if they've still got that old TV set . . ." ■

Continued from page 69

"Yes." He sniffed. "It is. Hey, I should have thought of that. I'm the writer, not you! I'll remember it, though."

Looking at his concentrated face, as he sniffed the woody smell, I knew he would.

We went on through the woods, and it grew warmer and I took off my mac. I slung it over my shoudlers, and unfastened my pigtails, wanting to feel the sun on my hair.

He looked at me appraisingly.

"That's better," he said, and I flushed, wondering if I shouldn't have kept it done up in the brown ribbon.

He was looking at me with different eyes now, and hastily I said the first thing I could think of.

"I'm hungry."

"So am I. I've got a couple of apples and some toast and marmalade I pinched at breakfast."

Joe grinned, and fishing out two small green apples from the pocket of his jeans, he offered one to me.

"Want one?" he repeated, and I took it, rubbing it on my gym slip till it shone, rivalling the green leaves on the trees.

"Jen, will you be an artist?" He bit deeply into the apple and crunched happily, and I looked back at him, envying his freedom. He was a boy, he could leave home and do whatever he wanted.

"I don't know. It's so difficult," I said dismally.

"Not if you really want to," he said firmly. "If you *really* want to do something you've got to do it. You can't let them push you into doing something else. You'd never be happy."

"No. But Aunt Jessie's done a lot for me. She'd like me to be a teacher," I added dolefully.

"Well," he said firmly. "If I can be a writer I'm sure you can be an artist. If you're any good. All you've got to do is make up your mind." He squinted through the bare branches at the sun, palely golden now. "Wonder what the time is?"

"Ten to twelve," I said, and took off my watch, absent-mindedly winding it. He glanced at it.

"That's nice. I never had a watch."

"Didn't you?"

★ ★ ★ ★

I couldn't imagine anyone not ever having a watch. My day seemed to be split up by that watch, the minute hand rushing round faster than I wanted it to when I was happy; slower than I could dream of when I was miserable. I held it out to him.

"It was my mother's. It's gold."

He took it admiringly, smoothing the delicate watch face with long grubby fingers.

"Pretty. You're lucky, Jen."

No-one, I thought, with a warm feeling, had ever called me Jen before. It was always Jennifer.

He got up abruptly, holding out the watch to me. "We've spent so long here we won't get much time at the river. We'll have your chocolate when we get there."

I was annoyed. It was my chocolate, and he'd taken charge of it, along with my currant bun. The chocolate, it seemed, was for now, while the bun was our tea-time treat.

I picked up my satchel wearily, sighing. I was getting tired, and it was colder, the sun disappearing behind the trees.

"I'll take it," he said abruptly, and took it from me, throwing it across his shoulders. "Come on. It'll be warmer at the river."

It was. There was a clearing on the river bank where the sun streaked warmly yellow, and the grass was dry and spiky and smelt like new-mown hay. Ducks quarrelled noisily on the bank.

I leaned back on the grass, head on my mac, and rolled up the sleeves of my brown cardigan, aware that he was looking down at me with a curious expression in his eyes. I hesitated. Something was missing.

"My watch!" I was filled with sheer unreasoning panic. "My watch! It's gone!" I glared accusingly up at him. He'd had it last, he couldn't have given it back to me.

"What?" He still stared at me, and I sat up angrily.

"My watch! What have you done with it?"

"Nothing! I haven't touched it, if that's what you're thinking!"

He was growing angry himself. "I gave it back to you!"

"You didn't! You didn't!" What could I do? Aunt Jessie would see it was gone the moment I walked in. And besides, it had been my mother's, the only thing I had left of hers.

He got up, showering me with tiny leaves and twigs. "You must have forgotten to put it on. You probably left it there in the clearing."

"I didn't! I wouldn't!" I was crying now, and he stood angrily glowering down at me.

PHANTOM?

All my housework was done and no-one was in the house as I lay relaxing on the sofa.

Suddenly the piano in the empty back room began to play.

I froze in horror. Eventually I plucked up enough courage to investigate.

The mystery pianist? Our cat! He was walking from the top to the bottom and sitting down occasionally for a rest.

I've never been so glad to see that old cat!

"I haven't stolen it." He spoke very clearly.
"I didn't say you had," I began, flushing miserably, but he was storming back into the woods.
"I'll go and find it," he called back to me. "Stay there or you'll get lost."
"Oh, wait!" I cried, but he'd gone, and I was alone on the edge of the river, and I was scared.
"Joe! Please, Joe! Let me come with you!"

HE didn't answer. I heard twigs crackling as he went swiftly away from me. I had a dreadful feeling that he'd never come back. He'd stolen my watch, and now he was running away with it.
Tears streaming down my cheeks, I stumbled after him. I'd follow him, find out where he lived, go to the police.
I fell once, into a deep hollow, lined with many years' accumulation of leaves, and it was soft and warm and damp, and I lay there for a moment, weakly sobbing.
I was lost. I'd have to try and get back to where I'd left my mac.
"Joe! Joe!" I began calling helplessly. I fell over a hidden branch, and caught my leg on a sharp pointed twig. I saw blood oozing. I felt a little sick, and the sun had gone in.
There was late afternoon chill in the air, and a little mist drifted lazily across the tree trunks. I wondered whether I would die of cold, alone out here all night.
I stumbled through the woods, and they weren't friendly any more. They seemed forbidding, alien, and I realised it was Joe who had brought them to life, telling me names of birds, pointing out the playing squirrels, finding hazelnuts for us to crack and crunch, hard and slightly bitter between our teeth.
"Joe!" I called out again. "Oh, Joe!" I was stumbling forward — then I stopped and stared, filled with fright, at the tall figure coming towards me.
"Joe!"
I ran towards him, satchel banging against my legs, arms goose-pimpled, wondering whether I should ever find my mac again, and what Aunt Jessie would say. Then I saw he had it over his shoulder.
"Jen!" He sounded furiously angry, his face was smudged with dirty streaks, and his hair ruffled. "Where did you get to? You stupid idiot! I told you to stay there!"
"I got lost," I faltered, and he flung my mac round my shoulders, forcing my shaking hands into the sleeves, buttoning it up under my chin as though I were five instead of fifteen.
"I can manage!" I said crossly, trying to hide the tears which had dried uncomfortably salty on my face. But he'd seen them.
"Scared, were you? Did you think I'd gone and left you?"
"I don't know," I stammered, and he abruptly dangled something shining and golden in front of me.
"My watch! Oh, Joe, you found it!"

"You thought I'd pinched it, didn't you?" he said matter of factly, and my cheeks were burning as I fumbled, strapping it round my wrist.

"You left it on the ground, where you were sitting by the sett. I had a job to find it."

I thought of him scrabbling through the leaves, turning over twigs. He'd got earth all over his jeans, and torn the back of his brave blue sweater.

"Oh, Joe." I stared up at him in the darkening wood. "I'm sorry."

He shrugged. " 'S all right. Anyway, I found you something."

He held out his other hand, and in it were three primroses.

"Go on, take them."

I hesitated.

"No. I got them for you. It's your birthday." Abruptly he leaned forward and kissed me, his lips touching mine fleetingly.

"It's all I've got to give you. Happy birthday, Jen."

We walked back along the river bank. At the edge of the woods, Joe turned, grinning down at me.

"I'll go and see you hanging in the Tate," he said, and I smiled a bit shakily at him.

"And I'll read your best-seller, too."

He shrugged. "Maybe. I'll be writing, anyway. See you."

With a casual wave he was gone.

I NEVER saw him again. Sometimes I wandered along to the council house estate where he'd said he lived, but the sight of the youths leaning against the walls with their hands in their pockets made me turn back.

But I got away. I fought for a place at the art school, and eventually I got my way. So I studied, and left home, and now I'm in London, in my studio flat, and I design textiles for a living, and paint for love.

Now, I look at the canvases propped around the walls, and I think, again, of Joe, and wonder what he looks like, and I stare down at the newspaper in my hand. The words leap out at me.

The Jungly Green Day, I read, and I'm fifteen again, sitting on the ground with Joe, smelling the soil and the freshness of spring.

The Jungly Green Day. An evocative short play from a new author. First love at its most understanding, I read, and looked for the name of the author.

Joseph Smith is a promising new playwright with a new quality, feeling and sensitivity rarely found these days.

I glance at my watch, the same watch Joe stumbled through the woods to find, and I see it is nearly 9.15. The play begins at 9.30.

When it's finished, I resolve, I'll write to Joseph Smith, and find out whether he is my Joe.

I'm sure he is.

* **THE END** *

COMPLETE STORY BY PATRICIA JOHNSTONE

Whatever Will Katy Do Next?

Only one person knew the answer — that lovable schemer, Katy herself. And she was giving away nothing!

THE first time I saw Katy Ferguson she was standing outside my flat waiting for me to come home from work.

"You've come about the room, of course," I said. "How long have you been waiting here?"

"Since lunchtime." She flashed an infectious, sharing sort of smile.

"But I only put the notice up at the newsagent's at lunchtime."

"I know," she said. "But I couldn't risk having you let the room to someone else, could I?"

Katy was always like that. Once she had decided what she wanted to happen, nothing could stop her from making sure that it happened her way.

We introduced ourselves and I took her into the living-room. It had new curtains and ancient peeling wallpaper. There was only one armchair, which I had picked up at a sale.

"It's heaven, Jenny," Katy said.

"I'm going to fix it up, of course. I only moved in two weeks ago."

"We'll begin with a coat of paint," Katy said, "after we've stripped the wallpaper."

We went through the formality of looking at the two bedrooms. Mine had a new divan, and Katy's (yes, I knew even then that it was going to be hers) had no furniture at all.

"I'll soon see to that," she said.

We looked at the kitchen, which had a downtrodden, if not actually sordid, appearance. Katy paused.

"It's divine," she said at last.

"We need a pot plant at the window, something green and traily. And you know, Jenny, I do believe we could get those stains off the cooker and have it gleaming white."

It occurred to me for the first time that the cooker probably was white underneath. A lot of things were occurring to me — like the flat was really a palace, and Katy and I were old friends already.

And yet anyone could see that we were an oddly contrasting pair. She was small and fair haired and very good at decisions. I was tall with brownish hair, and no good at all at managing my life.

The only place where I seemed to have confidence was the office, where I handled all kinds of impersonal problems. I had been promoted to private secretary, and I planned to have a long-term career.

"Well, then," I said at last, "the room's yours if you want it."

She moved in the very next day. Katy was working, too, of course, but she seemed to have limitless time and energy.

Together we painted the entire flat and shopped for furniture bargains. She showed me how to make lightshades out of tiny coloured circles of cardboard, and the cooker became a fairly respectable white.

We put up shelves and posters and a big notice board to be used for messages and timetables and things like dentist appointments.

It seemed a little surprising that a girl as pretty as Katy should be free every night of the week. When she put up her collage, as she called it, I understood why.

The collage was a board covered with photographs of various sizes, and every single one was of Fred. There was Fred with his parents and Fred with a mob of schoolboys, Fred in a boat and Fred on a building site, and a lot of Fred with Katy.

Fred, she explained, was a history teacher. He lived in Wiltshire.

The building site was their future home, and they were going to be married as soon as they had built the house themselves. It looked as though they had a good long way to go yet.

"It all sounds lovely," I said. She gave me her enquiring, how-about-you? look, and so I added, "Personally, I don't plan to get married."

Katy smiled.

"I mean it. I have this flat and my career, and a lot of things I'm interested in, and that's quite enough."

Katy said nothing.

WE were sitting in the living-room, having our late-night cocoa. There was a warm confidential feeling in the room.

Quite soon I was saying, "Actually, I did once plan to marry. His name was Larry and I thought I was in love with him. But . . . things didn't work out too well. So I came to London instead. And I've been perfectly happy ever since."

I didn't tell her how shattering that broken romance had been. I said nothing about the kindness of my family, and the good friends at home who had tried to keep me busy. It was still oddly painful to remember.

In a way, I had minded the blind dates more than anything. They were kindly meant, but they only confirmed that I was the leftover half of a twosome, a girl all alone.

"Of course you'll get married," Katy said. "Some man will find you and grab you."

"You have to be joking." I had no illusions at all about my grabability rating — zero. Larry had made that quite clear.

"Jenny," she said, "I think you ought to have your hair a bit shorter. And I'm not sure that flat heels really suit you. We want to bring out your height instead of trying to disguise it . . ."

That's how it went. Once the flat was completely organised, Katy started on me. And once she had decided on some improvement in my appearance, I meekly went ahead and improved.

Fred came to London every second Saturday, and Katy went to see him in Wiltshire on the alternate Saturdays. Soon he was like an old friend of mine, too.

It was a good arrangement. The flat would bustle with activity one weekend, and I had it peacefully all to myself the next.

Then came the Saturday when Fred brought Peter. I could tell by Katy's uncharacteristic meekness that Peter had been organised into coming.

"I'll go and put the kettle on," she said as soon as they arrived.

"Peter's a riding instructor," Fred told me. "He teaches some of the kids at my school. You ever done any riding, Jenny?"

"Not since I came to London." Katy knew perfectly well that back home, where we lived on the edge of the country, I had loved to go riding.

I noticed, with grudging respect for her ability, that Peter was exactly right. Katy's choices always were. There was a free and easy niceness about him, and the gentle good manners that very tall men sometimes have.

My own height seemed nothing beside his.

Katy brought out my favourite shortbread with the tea. Peter ate four pieces.

"I just can't resist it," he said. It would not have surprised me to learn that he used my brand of toothpaste, too.

It turned out that Fred and Katy had to go to Camden Town to look at insulating material for their house.

"You won't want to come with us, Peter," Katy said. "It's terribly boring." She prodded me with her eyes.

I said, "I have a lot of chores in the flat this morning. And I'll be shopping this afternoon."

Katy was going to have to learn. There was just one matter on which I would *not* be prodded. She could organise me and my flat and anything else she liked, but she was not going to arrange a single date for me. I was determined about that.

Peter said after a short hesitation, "Reckon I'll take the chance to do a few errands myself."

It was agreed that everyone would be back at the flat by five o'clock. Katy gave me a sideways look as she left, and I knew that the battle was on.

But I could hardly have guessed how swiftly she would rally.

★ ★ ★ ★

When I came back to the flat from my afternoon's shopping, there was a message from her on the noticeboard. It was scrawled on bright green paper to be sure I didn't miss it.

Desperately sorry. Involved with friends until after dinner. Please look after Peter.

I threw it into the kitchen bin. Katy, I was fairly sure, had never been desperately sorry for anything in her life.

Peter arrived at two minutes past five. He had the glazed look of a man who had been killing time for hours. I retrieved the note from the bin to show him. I did not want him to suppose that I was actually an accomplice in Katy's schemes.

He looked at the note with some surprise. There was a piece of tomato stuck on it from the bin. Then he stood up to his nice full height.

"In that case," he said, "we might find ourselves a place to have dinner . . . if that's OK?"

He could hardly have said less under the circumstances.

"Or we could hunt around for something to eat in the kitchen." I could hardly have said less either.

He grinned. "Let's go out, and you can show me your favourite restaurant."

Continued on page 82

WHEN we lived in a Midlands city, I often used to say we ought to keep a cow. The amount of milk our three children drank! But I never really meant it.

However, the day came when we moved to Devon and, because the children wanted a pony, we had to have a house with a field.

It didn't take us long to settle into country life and feel an integral part of the farming community. And I soon began to enjoy attending farm sales. It was at one of these that I met Sally.

There was a label stuck on her rump which bore the number 21. The catalogue merely stated she was a fifteen-month-old Guernsey heifer but the moment I saw her I knew her name was Sally. She just looked like a Sally — sweet, enchanting and rather mischievous, with a pair of violet eyes framed in a golden-brown face.

Of course, I didn't mean to actually buy a cow. I'd never milked one in my life and knew next to nothing about them. But, suddenly, there was this dainty, golden-haired angel being led into the auction ring and, before I knew where I was, I'd bought her for twenty-five pounds.

Getting her home wasn't difficult. We only lived three miles away and a friend kindly transported her.

There, Sally was quickly settled into an old cowshed, introduced to Tommy, the skewbald pony, and voted one of the family.

Sally, however, had other ideas. She wasn't used to being isolated from other cows. She had been a member of a herd and a member of a herd she again intended to be!

She was perfectly sweet tempered, never kicked and only playfully butted us. But the moment she was let out into the field she'd find a gap in the hedge, struggle through it and was off in search of bovine companions.

PERSONALITY PETS

SALLY

OUR HAPPY LITTLE WANDERER

BY MRS N. SMITH

F

Day after exasperating day, my husband or I had to go in search of her. We'd chase her up hills and down roads, through mud and across streams.

During one such excursion we found Sally visiting a smallholding a mile away. So while I drove the car slowly behind, my poor husband half-pulled, half-pushed that unwilling animal homewards.

Two days later, believe it or not, the entire herd of thirteen cows that Sally had visited arrived at our field gate. They had decided to return the compliment!

BUT there was never any suggestion of re-selling Sally. She was a real pet. She learned her name quickly and when it was feed time she would come when called. When it wasn't, she would just turn her head, look at us as though to say — "I don't want to come now" — and continue nibbling the grass or hedgerow.

Soon the time arrived to put her in calf. This procedure went quite smoothly and in due course we were thrilled to know she was to become a mum. And from that moment, Sally began to behave more sedately, as befitted a matron.

Then one hot, thundery August day she showed a distinct reluctance to eat her breakfast and leave the cowshed. I shoved her out but returned later to see if she was all right. I found her lying down. It was obvious motherhood was imminent.

I quickly called the children, and all four of us stood at a distance and watched, utterly enthralled, as Sally's baby was born.

Ten minutes later, as thunder rumbled across the sky, the little dark-haired calf struggled to her feet. Staggering and stumbling like a drunk, she swayed and finally stood and surveyed the strange world she had so recently entered.

And, of course, as the thunder continued to rumble ominously, we decided to name the baby Thunder.

★ ★ ★ ★

When it came to milking her, Sally stood quiet and patient while first my husband and then myself slowly and gently learned to hand-milk.
Although she never kicked or actually misbehaved, it seemed she couldn't resist a quick flick of her tail into an unwary face bent over the milk-pail.

She was intelligent, too. No matter how we tied the cow-chain around her neck, whenever she wanted to, she could get free. She'd twist and wriggle, and thrust her head between the stall-bars until she'd pulled the chain victoriously over her head.

To the local farmers, of course, she was just another cow but Sally was much more than that to us. She was a pet, a favourite member of our ever-growing family of animals and a character we'll never forget. ■

Continued from page 80

HARDENING my heart against the beguiling idea that I actually had a favourite restaurant, I took him to Sam's Eating House on the corner near the main road.

Katy might think she was winning, but she would have to admit that a meal at Sam's didn't count as a date. The big attraction, for Sam's patrons, was the low prices. It had a heady atmosphere of smoke and oil and ketchup, and there was a vintage juke-box that played the hits of yesteryear.

Peter cornered an almost clean table, and we sat on opposite sides with a tin ashtray between us. He ordered grills for two with every appearance of enjoyment. And calmly chattered about his horses and about how he liked to go fishing on Sundays.

I switched the conversation to Bingo, ballroom dancing and zoos, all of which I detest. Even so, we came dangerously close to agreeing when he threw out some ideas for the reformation of zoos. It was, in fact, difficult to find a subject on which we had no sort of agreement.

He began to look puzzled. Eventually silence overtook us. We went home early. We were reading magazines in the flat when Katy and Fred arrived back.

As soon as we were alone together Katy turned on me accusingly.

"Jenny, you just didn't try to get on with Peter."

"That's right, I didn't."

"Didn't you like him at all?"

"That's not the point. The point is that I *hate* any kind of blind date. I always have and always will."

Katy looked thoughtful. I supposed, at the time, that she was considering my point of view.

As it turned out, I supposed wrong.

On a Saturday two weeks later, when she and Fred were busy somewhere in London, I came home to the flat in the afternoon and found another bright green note on the board.

Delayed until after dinner. Be an angel and look after our friend Jules if he arrives.

"*If* he arrives . . ." I muttered on my way to the bin. With Katy to do the masterminding, every detail would be correct.

There was a smart rap at the door. Jules turned out to be tall, dark-eyed and gallant.

He had recently arrived to teach French at that school of Fred's in Wiltshire. He was longing to see London.

I took him to Sam's Eating House.

It was an instant success. He assumed that he was seeing life as the Britishers live it — the real thing, not just for tourists. Sam's patrons loved him.

He greeted them all in French and they called back to him in colloquial English.

When Katy and Fred arrived at the flat we were drinking Fred's wine.

" 'Allo!" Jules cried, "Ve 've a smashing time. Ve ate bangers and mash, innit luv?"

With Katy's sharp gaze on me I admitted that we had.

Later, when Fred had finally dragged Jules off to Wiltshire, Katy fetched our cocoa from the kitchen.

"Jenny, how *could* you take Jules to Sam's?"

"It was a bad mistake," I admitted. "He loved the place."

"Bangers and mash," Katy moaned.

"Katy, you have got to stop organising dates for me."

"But you won't even try to meet any nice men by yourself."

"That's right," I agreed. "And it would save a lot of trouble if you'd stop trying to make me meet them."

"I can't," she said frankly. "I've already arranged for Fred to bring

Continued on page 90

THE CHOICE IS CHICKEN!

A popular bird with gourmets all over the world. Here are some unusually tasty recipes to tickle your palate . . .

ROAST CHICKEN WITH APPLE AND SAGE SAUCE

1 green-skinned eating apple
12 cloves
1 x 3½ lb./1.5 kg British chicken, prepared for cooking
4 to 6 small sprigs fresh sage
12 fl. oz./360 ml chicken stock
3 tablespoonfuls thick natural yoghurt
1 egg yolk
1 teaspoonful cornflour, slackened with 2 tablespoonfuls water
1 tablespoonful brandy
Salt and freshly-ground black pepper

Garnish:
3 green-skinned eating apples
4 tablespoonfuls crab apple jelly (or other fruit jelly)
4 fl. oz./120 ml dry cider, or water
Sprigs fresh sage

Halve, core and quarter the apples; spike each quarter with a few cloves. Stuff the chicken with half the sage and the spiked apples, and place in a deep ovenproof dish; add the stock and the remaining sage.

Cover with foil and cook at 375 deg. F., 190 deg. C., Gas Mark 5, for 45 minutes; remove the foil, baste the bird and cook for a further 45 minutes, uncovered, or until the chicken is tender. Keep the bird warm.

Strain the chicken stock into a measuring jug and make up to ⅓ pint/200 ml with water, if necessary. Mix the yoghurt, egg and slackened cornflour together and add 2 tablespoonfuls of the chicken stock.

Heat the remaining measured stock in a saucepan; add the blended cornflour mixture and stir over a gentle heat until the sauce has thickened. Add the brandy and salt and pepper to taste, and a little extra chopped fresh sage, if liked. (This gives a more prominent flavour to the sauce.)

Carve or joint the chicken, and serve with the stuffed apple halves (see below), the prepared sauce and a few sprigs sage.

To prepare the stuffed apple halves:

Cut each apple in half crossways; carefully scoop out the core from each apple half, leaving a "shell" about ½ inch/1 cm thick. Stand upright in an ovenproof dish and fill the hollows with crab apple jelly; spoon the cider around the apples. Cook in the oven with the chicken for the last 15 minutes. ***Serves 6.***

Calories per portion 272.

CHICKEN TACOS

2 tablespoonfuls thick natural yoghurt
1½ tablespoonfuls milk
3 teaspoonfuls chopped fresh chives

Salt and freshly-ground black pepper
4 taco shells
6 tablespoonfuls finely-shredded lettuce
8 oz./225 g cooked British chicken, finely chopped
½ a red pepper, seeded and finely chopped
½ a green pepper, seeded and finely chopped
Sprigs fresh herbs or parsley to garnish

Mix the yoghurt, milk and half the chives together and season to taste with salt and pepper.

Warm the taco shells through, curved sides uppermost, in the oven (350 deg. F., 180 deg. C., Gas Mark 4) for 4 minutes.

Fill each taco shell with alternate layers of lettuce, chicken and red and green pepper.

Carefully spoon the yoghurt sauce over the taco filling and sprinkle with the remaining chopped chives. Serve immediately with a bean salad.

Note: Have all filling ingredients ready so that the tacos can be assembled quickly, while the shells are still warm.

Serves 4.

Calories per portion 150.

CHICKEN STRIPS with WALNUTS

4 boneless breasts of Quality British Chicken, skinned
6 tablespoonfuls walnut oil
3 tablespoonfuls vodka
Salt and black pepper
1 oz. toasted walnut halves
Lemon juice, to taste
1 lb. tomatoes, very thinly sliced
2 cloves garlic, finely chopped
2 tablespoonfuls chopped parsley

Cut each chicken breast lengthwise into 3 even pieces. Place these with 2 tablespoonfuls of the oil and the vodka in a shallow dish. Season with salt and pepper, to taste.

Cover the dish and chill on lowest shelf of refrigerator for at least 2 hours.

Heat a frying-pan and cook the chicken with the marinade until the chicken is just cooked through. Add the walnut halves, 1 tablespoonful of the oil and the lemon juice. Check seasoning and cook for 3-4 minutes, being careful not to over-cook.

Arrange overlapping slices of tomatoes in a shallow serving dish. Sprinkle with the remaining oil, garlic, parsley and seasoning to taste. Cover and chill until ready to serve.

Spoon the hot chicken, walnuts and juices over the cold tomatoes and serve with a sprinkling of chopped parsley, if liked. ***Serves 4.***

About 380 calories per portion.

CHICKEN and APPLE HASH

2 tablespoonfuls oil
1 medium onion, finely chopped
2 medium leeks, split, cleaned and shredded
8 fl. oz. chicken stock
2 teaspoonfuls soya sauce
1 teaspoonful lemon juice
Salt and black pepper
1 teaspoonful cornflour
1 egg yolk
4 tablespoonfuls thick natural yoghurt
½ cold, cooked British chicken cut, into strips
1 large eating apple, thinly sliced

Heat the oil in a large shallow pan and fry the onion gently for 2 minutes. Add the leeks and fry for 2 minutes more. Add the stock and bubble briskly until reduced by a third.

Add soya sauce, lemon juice and seasoning to taste.

Mix the cornflour with 1 tablespoonful of water, then blend with the egg yolk and yoghurt. Stir into the stock and allow to thicken over a gentle heat.

Add the chicken and apple slices and heat through gently to soften the apple very slightly. Serve with Curried Oven Fries (see recipe) and garnish with chopped chives, if liked. *Serves 4.*

About 235 calories per portion.

CURRIED OVEN FRIES

4 medium potatoes, peeled
3 tablespoonfuls oil
1-2 teaspoonfuls curry powder
Salt and black pepper

Cut the potatoes in half lengthways, then cut each half into 4 or 5 even, wedge-shaped pieces. Using a large fluted pastry cutter, cut along the curved edge of each potato wedge.

Put the oil in a shallow ovenproof dish and heat through at 375 deg. F., 190 deg. C., Gas Mark 5, for 3 minutes.

Pat the fluted potato wedges dry on absorbent paper and add to the hot oil. Stir to coat evenly. Cook for 15 minutes.

Turn the potato wedges and sprinkle with curry powder and seasoning to taste. Return to the oven for 20-25 minutes until crisp and golden brown.

Serve with the Chicken and Apple Hash. *Serves 4.*

About 114 calories per portion.

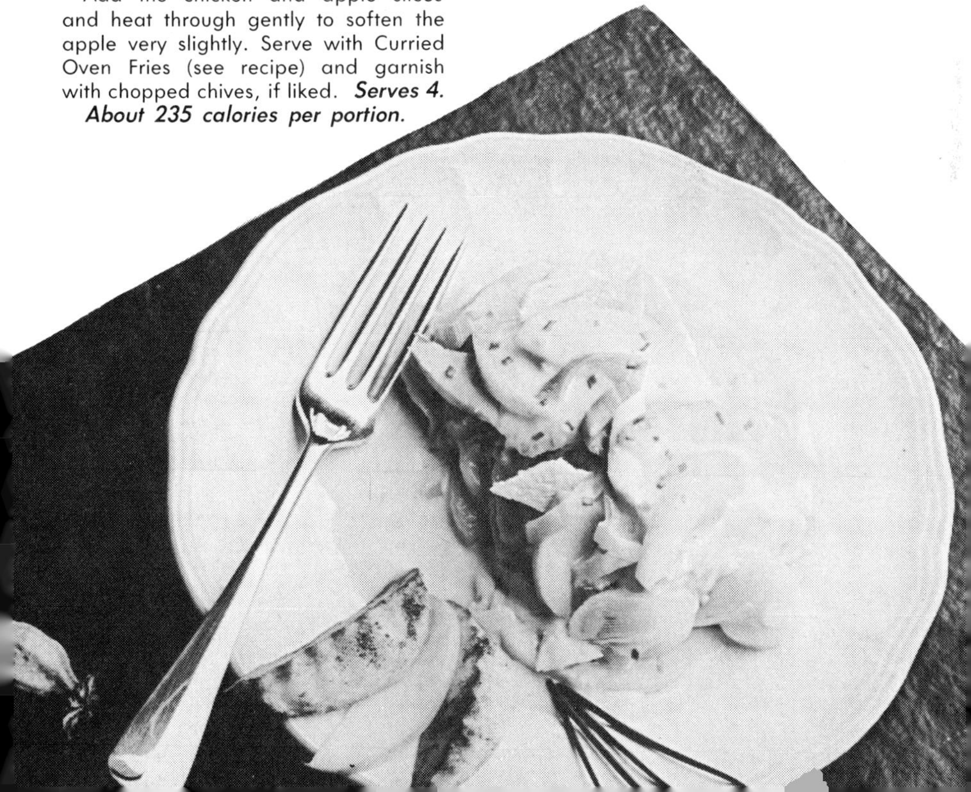

ROAST CHICKEN WITH WALNUT AND PEAR STUFFING

1 small ripe pear, cored and chopped (about ¼ inch/½ cm)
2 oz./50 g wholemeal breadcrumbs
1 oz./25 g chopped walnuts
Generous pinch ground ginger
Salt and freshly-ground black pepper
1 egg yolk
5 cloves
½ lemon
1 x 3½ lb./1.5 kg British chicken, prepared for cooking
2 tablespoonfuls clear honey

Garnish:
1 pear, cored and sliced
1 tablespoonful clear honey

Mix the chopped pear with the breadcrumbs, walnuts, ginger and salt and pepper to taste; mix in the egg yolk.

Push the cloves into the skin of the half lemon and place inside the chicken. Press the pear stuffing into the neck cavity of the chicken and fold the remaining neck skin underneath the bird, to secure the stuffing.

Place the chicken in a roasting dish, season with salt and pepper and brush

all over with the honey. Cook in the oven at 400 deg. F., 200 deg. C., Gas Mark 6, for 1¼ to 1½ hours.

Spoon the melted honey over the bird 2 or 3 times during cooking. (The chicken juices should run clear when the thickest part of the leg is pierced with a fine skewer.) If the chicken darkens too much during cooking, cover it with a piece of foil or double thickness greaseproof paper.

To prepare the glazed pears for garnish:

Put the sliced pears into a pan with the honey; stir over a gentle heat, turning the pears from time to time until they become translucent. Carve or joint the chicken and serve with the glazed pears. ***Serves 6.***

Calories per portion 284.

FLORIDA CHICKEN

3½ lb. British chicken, prepared for cooking
½ pint orange juice
1 pint chicken stock
Juice 2 lemons
4 teaspoonfuls finely-chopped fresh tarragon (or 1 teaspoonful dried chopped tarragon)
Salt and black pepper
4 tablespoonfuls thick natural yoghurt
4 tablespoonfuls low-calorie mayonnaise
Juice and grated rind of ½ orange
1 whole orange

Put the chicken into a large pan with the orange juice, stock, lemon juice, half the tarragon and seasoning to taste.

Cover and bring to the boil. Simmer gently for 1½ hours until the chicken is tender. Drain, reserving the poaching liquid. Leave the chicken to cool.

Mix the yoghurt with the mayonnaise, half the remaining tarragon, 3 tablespoonfuls of the poaching juices, grated orange rind and juice and seasoning to taste.

Carve the chicken and arrange on a flat platter. Remove all peel and pith from the whole orange and divide into segments. Carefully spoon the yoghurt sauce evenly over the chicken and sprinkle with remaining chopped tarragon. Garnish with peeled orange segments and sprigs of fresh tarragon if available. ***Serves 6.***

About 250 calories per portion.

Note — The leftover poaching liquid can be used for cooking vegetables, in casseroles, etc.

SPICY PILAFF

3 tablespoonfuls Kraft Italian Garlic Dressing
1 teaspoonful tandoori spice mixture
1 teaspoonful dried oregano
1 lb. boneless chicken breast, cut into strips
3 oz. mushrooms, chopped
1 small green pepper, sliced
1 medium onion, chopped
8 oz. cooked brown rice

In a bowl mix the dressing, tandoori spice and oregano. Coat the chicken in this mixture and leave for at least 3 hours or preferably overnight.

In a large non-stick frying-pan, cook the chicken for 7-10 minutes. Add the mushrooms, green pepper and onion, cook for 2-3 minutes. Add the rice and cook, stirring gently, for a further 5-7 minutes.

Serve immediately. ***Serves 4.***

400 calories per portion.

Continued from page 83
his cousin Anthony next time he comes to London. He breeds dogs in Dorset, you know."

I put down my cocoa in indignant silence.

"Jenny, you *know* you like dogs. You told me about the time your Labrador had puppies."

I sighed. "All right, I like dogs. Only . . . no more dates. Promise you won't leave any more of those ghastly notes."

She gave me a long, clear look. "I promise."

ANTHONY came. He brought an Alsatian puppy to show to someone in London.

He was as good natured as the puppy, and even I couldn't prevent the lunch that Katy and I cooked from being a riotous success. I had planned to wash my hair that afternoon, but I went with Anthony and the puppy to Wimbledon instead, to see its prospective owners.

When we came back the flat was empty. I scanned the noticeboard. It was innocent of green notes.

Then the telephone rang. It was Katy, keeping to the narrow terms of her promise. She told me, without a hint of embarrassment, that she and Fred would be detained until nine that evening.

Anthony insisted on taking me out to dinner. It took all my resolution to inflict Sam's on him, when he so clearly deserved something better.

Even so, the dinner was nearly a success. He thought it was terribly funny to have come all the way from Dorset to a place exactly like his nearest roadhouse at home. He saved the toughest parts of our steaks for the puppy, which had not been sold.

"Katy," I said when the flat was quiet again, "this has to be the last time. We can't go on like this."

"It was rotten of you to go and do the washing up while Anthony and Fred were still here."

"Yes, I know it was. But you've got to stop organising dates for me. It'll never be any good."

There was a long silence. "All right," she said soberly. "You win. Tonight was the last time."

THE following Saturday Katy took a train to Wiltshire. She brought me coffee in bed before leaving. "And Fred isn't bringing anyone else next week," she said virtuously.

"Good." I stretched luxuriously in bed.

Perhaps I had been too harsh with Katy. She had meant so well. Anyway it was all over now, and I had a peaceful day ahead.

It certainly was peaceful. I tidied the flat. I washed my hair. I turned on the radio. I hunted out library books and some old knitting. And still the hours stretched out ahead.

It was a fine thing, I kept thinking, to have a job that I liked. But on an empty Saturday, surely I should have something better to do than just wait for Monday morning to come around again.

What about my own interests then? But they all centred around home — things like a dog I once had, and a country lane where I used to go riding. I was hit by a wave of homesickness.

I thought about my family and friends I hadn't seen in a long time. Hadn't wanted to see because of painful memories. Carefully, I thought about the shattered romance. The old familiar pain didn't come. Had I really recovered?

Yes. Thanks to Katy, my vanity had recovered. And now I could understand that nothing else had ever been hurt. It was a simple case of pride. And I had been too proud to accept all the blind dates and the good times she had offered.

Guiltily, I thought about Jules and his irrepressible fun, Anthony protecting his puppy . . . I had been too concerned with my own stupid pride to enjoy all that.

I thought about Peter, big and gentle, telling me about his horses. The way his eyes grew puzzled when I didn't respond.

And there it was — a pang of pure pain.

I DON'T remember deciding to go out.

I remember walking in a drizzle, going along our block and around a few others, with no ideas at all in my mind. The pain, like a toothache, wouldn't quite subside.

After a while I stopped at a lighted window. I wasn't noticing much. It was the familiar blend of smells that told me where I was.

The attraction at Sam's wasn't only the low prices. I had been wrong about that. There was warmth in here, warmth and humanity.

The girl at the counter said in a puzzled voice, "Isn't that your friend, luv?"

I looked over to the corner. A big man in a sheepskin jacket looked up gloomily from a half-empty cup.

"Peter!" I cried joyfully.

He saw me and gave me a subdued grin. Someone moved up and a chair was wedged in for me next to Peter.

"Jenny," he said, and his grin broadened.

"I know that Katy must have organised you into coming . . ."

"This is one time that Katy didn't organise anything," he said. "I came up to see you today because I knew she wouldn't be in. Only I didn't know your phone number either.

"Then I started thinking that you wouldn't be too pleased to see me."

He looked down at the table, and then straight into my eyes. "You didn't enjoy being with me last time."

"Can't we forget about last time?"

He looked at me carefully. The happiness must have shown in my face, because at last he gave a satisfied nod.

"Yes," he said. "I think we can."

*** THE END ***

The Letter

It took only a few moments to write — but it was enough to save two people from years of unhappiness.

I CALLED at my daughter's house on my way to town to return some preserving jars she had lent me, and because I thought we might snatch a cup of coffee together before I went on my usual Friday shopping trip. Joanne only worked part-time, in the afternoons.

There was no reply when I rang so I put down the carrier bag and felt for the spare key in my handbag. She had given it to me for emergencies years ago and told me to use it when I called, but I didn't like to in the normal way.

I wouldn't have wanted anyone walking in on a row or a private moment, and I wouldn't do it to Joanne. However, I didn't want to

Complete Story by DOROTHY L. GARRARD

carry the jars into town, so I unlocked her yellow front door and stepped into the cool hall.

Inside, there were two very large suitcases, a hold-all, and Joanne's roomy beach bag, standing by the door. I felt surprised, and absurd disappointment.

Joanne hadn't told me they were going away. I understood they'd booked their holidays for late September at Ben's favourite hotel in Devon.

"Joanne?" I called. "Jo? Anybody there?"

There was no reply. The lounge door was wide open, and the room, newly cleaned and polished, looked strangely bare without

Ben's perpetual litter of newspapers and signs of his several hobbies all over the place.

I glanced at the clock. It was a moment before I realised what was wrong, then I saw that Joanne's little ornaments, which she treasured as souvenirs from school journeys years ago, were missing.

SHE would want the jars in the kitchenette, I decided. I walked through the dining-room to get to it, and I saw that a clean cloth was spread on the table with a place laid for one. It was a dinner place, with steak knife, fork and spoon, and the large striped breakfast cup Ben insisted on using whatever the meal or the colour of the rest of the crockery.

When they had guests, Joanne hid it away so he couldn't find it. I smiled and shook my head. Ben was so very like Dick, my husband — say what you like and they blandly listened and then ignored it.

In fact, Ben was so like Dick that it had been almost amusing the first time Joanne had brought him home. I'd felt so at home with him, as if he was already familiar. He had the same big build, was a little clumsy, and considered his words before he spoke.

He even had the same sense of humour. Subtlety didn't raise more than a faint smile, but custard pie slapstick would have him rocking in his chair and bellowing with laughter.

One night when I remarked on this likeness to Joanne she'd looked a bit startled, and then said, "Well, yes, I see what you mean. The same type as Dad, I suppose."

When they became engaged the following June, there was only one thing which worried me, and I had to mention it. Joanne didn't tell me everything and I wouldn't have wanted her to, but we had a close and reasonably frank relationship which allowed me to say, "Jo, you know I'm very fond of Ben. But are you quite sure you're not settling for a . . . father figure?"

She gave me a quizzical glance. "I know he's six years older than I am, Mum, but I wouldn't call him that — not the way I feel about him! But even if I was — I could do worse, couldn't I?"

It was the first time she had referred, even obliquely, to that disastrous romance with Roy Blake several years ago. It had been a long time before she accepted any more dates, and Ben was the only man she had ever brought home since Roy.

I took the reference to Roy as a good omen. For a long time the mere mention of anything even vaguely related to him would bring a haggard look to her face and anguished tears to her eyes.

If she was happy again, then so was I. And as for Dick, he already regarded Ben as one of the family and it would have been distinctly embarrassing if Jo had ever broken off the relationship.

I CAME out of my reverie to find myself still standing in the quiet house — a home now, with several years of living behind it. In the spick and span kitchenette the cooker was set on automatic, and a casserole was visible through the glass-fronted oven.

I put the bag with the jars in it on to the kitchen chair and went to the back door. It was bolted, so Joanne wouldn't be in the garden.

I returned to the hall and looked again at the suitcases. Some vague unrest sent me slowly up the stairs, telling myself all the time not to be such a fool.

In their room the bed was neatly made, the dressing-table almost as bare as the mantelpiece. There were no make-up bottles or jewellery tray. The pretty dressing-table mats which I'd crocheted were gone.

In their place was a set from a chain store. A fearful intuition made me do what I'd never have done in normal circumstances — I opened the large double wardrobe door.

My mouth went dry. Ben's suits and shirts hung sedately on the rails, but none of Jo's clothes were there. Nor her shoes.

Trembling, I went slowly down the stairs again, wondering desperately what to do. What else could this mean — except that Joanne was leaving Ben.

Naturally, I would have dismissed it, except that I happened to know that Roy Blake had been back in town for several months.

I hadn't mentioned it to Joanne, but my closest friend, Louise Corrie, who lived near Roy's parents, had said he'd returned. He was, apparently, looking quite prosperous and about to open a new branch of his furnishing business in town.

Louise knew about Joanne's broken love affair with Roy, and was forthright in saying she'd been luckier than she knew. It appeared that Roy's marriage to the girl for whom he'd jilted Jo was on the rocks already.

Roy wasn't my type of person, but I had to admit that I could understand his physical attraction. He was slim, and quick to laugh.

His good looks and whirlwind courtship had held Jo a willing captive. But surely, I thought, after almost three years of marriage to a warm, affectionate, steady man like Ben . . .

I SWALLOWED a lump in my throat. I knew without being told that Joanne had never really forgotten Roy. She had been so desperately in love with him that she would have welcomed him back without question.

I remembered how, for almost a year after he left, she only seemed to come to life when the doorbell or the telephone rang.

Thinking of telephones, I looked at Joanne's and remembered that it had been out of order. I lifted it and listened. It was still dead.

Ben had the car for work, so Jo must have gone to the nearest call box to phone for a taxi to take her wherever she was going. She would be back any minute.

I wondered what do to — whether to go or stay and try to advise? But if Jo had made up her mind what could I possibly say that would make any difference?

Continued on page 97

LAURA OUR CRAZY MIXED UP PARROT

BY MRS M. E. REWE

PERSONALITY PETS

LAURA appeared one day, and by "appeared" I mean just that. One day I came in to lunch and there she sat on a large table in the corner of my grandmother's kitchen.

She was a large Amazon parrot with beautiful glossy green plumage which turned dark blue on the tips of her wings and lemon on her face.

She cocked one bright eye in my direction and it was love at first sight.

From that day on as soon as I entered the house Laura would scream for joy and leap up and down on her perch.

Then she would sidle along her perch and put her head on one side and croak and coo to me. I, in my turn, would tickle her and talk to her for hours until she became drowsy and curled up into a large green ball.

We were all surprised at Laura loving me so much because she was not normally a loving bird. In fact, with other people she was most aggressive and at times unpleasant!

Her first owner, an elderly lady, doted on her and allowed her as much freedom as possible. Laura was allowed to fly, walk, skip and hop all over the house, and she abused this trust by ferociously attacking any visitors who came to the house, then retreating under a chair and glaring at them balefully.

All would still have been well if Laura had not decided to "have a go" at her indulgent owner, who had the habit of holding a tit-bit in her mouth for Laura to take.

Laura had always been very good at doing this, but one day, instead of taking the tit-bit, Laura fastened her large horny beak over the lady's top lip and refused to let go!

It took several people a lot of time and care to get Laura to release her hold, but by that time, the old lady never wanted to see her again!

The next person to take on Laura was a kind-hearted person who was a great friend of my grandmother's.

She decided that Laura must stay in her cage for the safety of all concerned. Laura, needless to say, was extremely angry at this restriction to her liberty.

Despite the fact that the cage was very large, Laura repaid the lady's kindness by trying to bite her fingers, and anyone else's that she could reach through the bars.

My grandmother, who had always admired Laura, despite her rather vitriolic temper, said she would have her.

MY grandmother also had a beautiful tortoiseshell cat, which disliked Laura as much as Laura disliked her. The cat would spend hours thinking of ways to torment Laura.

One of her favourite tricks was to nonchalantly lay one brown velvet paw through the bars at the bottom of Laura's cage.

Laura, who was always on the top perch when this was done, would climb down laboriously to grab at the offending paw. But by the time she reached it it would have disappeared.

Laura would climb on to her perch and, in a rage, grab clawfuls of seed and hurl them through the bars.

Seed was not Laura's only food. Whenever my grandmother cooked chicken Laura would leap up and down until she was given a large piece. She would grasp it in one claw and daintily consume it.

Laura lived with us for many years and we were very shocked, one winter morning, when we found her gasping on the floor of her cage.

My grandmother, a very wise woman, swiftly picked her up and, wrapping her in a warm cloth, laid her gently in the warm oven.

The vet was called and diagnosed Laura's condition as pneumonia. He said she would stand greatest chance of recovery if she was left where she was.

So for three days Laura lived in the oven, coming out only at night when she was put into a warmly-lined box by the fire. At the end of the third day, a voice enquired coyly from the oven, "Laura go bye-byes!"

Laura survived and was able to amuse the whole neighbourhood as usual that summer with her screams for "Help!"

But, unfortunately, the following year the same thing happened and this time, despite all our care, Laura died.

We will always remember her with love and great pleasure, as I'm sure will all those who came into contact with her — even the ones who were bitten! ■

Continued from page 95

Tears sprang to my eyes as I saw the little carved box which Joanne kept on the small shelf by the front door. If she had taken such trifles as my crocheted mats, surely she wouldn't leave without slipping that box into her bulging beach bag?

The Memory Box, we called it when Dick had made it. He was normally no good with his hands — in fact, his ineptitude at knocking in a nail and his reluctance to handle any tools were a wry family joke.

But this box was special. He had carved it while a prisoner-of-war, doggedly chipping out a likeness of the cottage where he'd left me to wait for him, complete with roses round the door.

The rest of the box he had covered with souvenirs of home. A groggy-looking cat, a lop-sided retriever, flowers, birds, trees, a circular radiant sun, sweet images to a man longing for home. None of the likenesses were good, yet together they were charming.

He had brought it halfway across the world with him — because it had become a symbol of something he considered to be precious.

It took pride of place in our house and became the accepted receptacle for notes of all kinds. *Dick loves Laura,* he would write in the early days, and the joy of the reunion. Messages were left inside it and Joanne, as soon as she could write, followed suit.

It proved an unexpected bulwark against anxiety as she grew older, for habit became ingrained.

At the cinema with So and So, her notes would say, many a time when other parents would have been left to wonder.

We had made a gift of it to her when she moved, because Dick wanted to give his beloved only child a part of himself. And the box was the most personal thing he could give.

Quickly I tore a leaf from the telephone pad, picked up the pencil, and with fingers which would scarcely hold it steady I wrote:

Ben loves Joey — his pet name for her. Then I slipped it into the box, leaving a tiny corner showing.

I SHOPPED without really knowing what I bought, and went blindly about my housework when I returned. If only the phone hadn't been out of order . . .

Several times I got to the front door, then stopped. If Joanne had gone, there was nothing I could do. If she was still there, it was for Joanne and Ben to sort out first of all. She was his wife, and not my baby any more.

On tenterhooks I waited for seven-thirty, when Ben and Joanne usually came over. Dick looked forward to their company and I couldn't bear to imagine his dismay if they didn't come, or Ben came alone, and I had to tell him why.

Ben did come alone — but he looked his usual cheerful self.

"I won't be staying long tonight. Jo's in bed," he said. "Looks as if she'll be there for the weekend. I came home to find her all red eyed and bunged up with a streaming cold — a really romantic sight!"

I almost fainted with relief. With Ben around, she'd be safe for the weekend at any rate.

"I'd have rung you instead," Ben went on, "but the phone's still out of order and so's the box up the road. So I thought I might as well drop by."

I wondered how far Jo had gone to find a working telephone. Only to send the taxi away when it called? Or had she gone, and returned in the space of a few hours, for some reason only known to her and Roy? I wondered if I would ever know.

DICK always went fishing on Sundays. I phoned Joanne in the morning.

The telephone was working — I could hear the ringing tone — but no-one answered. I decided to go over that afternoon, but a bare ten minutes after I put the phone down Joanne walked in.

"Ben's cleaning the car and I felt like a walk," she said. She was pale and lacked sparkle, but there was no trace of a bad cold.

It seemed an effort for her to make conversation at first, and finally, over coffee, I said tentatively, "Is anything wrong, Joey?"

"You haven't called me that for years," she said, head bent over her cup.

"Not since you said it made you sound like a budgerigar!"

"That was because . . . Roy didn't like it. He said it was childish and I should grow up. I wonder what made you suddenly use it now?"

"Ben always calls you Joey," I said.

Slowly she raised her head and looked steadily at me. My memory of that awful Friday morning brought guilty colour to my face. I felt I had somehow confirmed Joanne's suspicions.

"Thanks for returning the jars," Jo said quietly.

I sat down suddenly and heavily. How could I have forgotten those jars? I'd left them there like a calling card and never given them another thought.

"Jo . . ." I began.

She silenced me with a quick gesture.

"No — don't say anything. I'd never have told you, except that you'd called, and must have guessed. It's a mistake I'll have to live with.

"But it wasn't the note that stopped me. I know Ben loves me and I care for him, too. Or why would I do a crazy thing like making sure his dinner would be ready on time, even though I wouldn't be there?"

Her eyes were wet. "It was when I picked up the box — before I saw the note. I thought quite clearly, Roy will laugh at me. Your pretty mats, Dad's box, my ornaments . . . none of them would have meant a thing to Roy.

"He said it was me he'd always loved, and we could take up where we left off. But he didn't know the real me at all. There's a part of me Roy never had time for, and all at once I realised what a big part it was.

"I'd have had to leave more behind than Ben, or you and Dad. He was always telling me to grow up, but when I finally did . . ."

She looked at me in silence, and I saw the completed sentence in her wet, shadowed eyes.

". . . when I did, I left Roy behind."

She blew her nose. "I've been a prisoner in my own home, the victim of an imaginary cold, to keep up appearances. All at once I feel free. Could I stay and have lunch with you?"

"Shall I ring Ben and tell him to come over?" I asked.

Something like a smile appeared in Joanne's eyes. "Well, I knew you wouldn't say no, so I left him a note. Just ring and tell him to look in the Memory Box."

*** THE END ***

COMPLETE
STORY
by SUSAN SALLIS

A Marriage Made In Heaven

TWO weeks before the wedding, on a windy, late winter's morning, another batch of presents arrived at the flat.

To Julie and Tom, read the little silver-printed cards inside.

They had a strange effect on Julie. Sitting at the breakfast table in her dressing-gown, her hair unkempt, and the parcels half-opened around her, she began to cry.

Peggy Russell reached across the marmalade and laid her hand on her daughter's.

"I can't go through with it, Mother," Julie said in a stifled voice. "I'll have to tell Tom it's no good."

Peggy withdrew her hand and tried to be objective. Tom and Julie were right for each other, she was sure. Then Julie's doubts and unhappiness could only be caused by one thing.

"Darling . . ." She heard her voice shake, as she searched for the right words. "Are you afraid that — that Tom might leave you, one day?"

Julie looked across at her mother with brutal honesty. "Like Daddy left us? Well, why not? I suppose you were both in love when you got married?"

Peggy flinched and turned away. She'd accepted that divorce had

That was how she wanted to think of her future. But hadn't she once thought that about her parents' marriage?

hardened her. But that it should have hardened Julie as well . . .

"But you and Tom are two different people."

Julie started putting the presents back into their boxes and said wearily in the words of all younger generations, "You don't understand, Mum. There's more to it than that."

She put the boxes on the sideboard with the others. "I'll have to tell Tom tonight."

Peggy watched her trail out of the kitchen and into the bathroom. She heard the bath water and listened for the usual tuneless hum that accompanied Julie's morning bath. It didn't come.

Peggy sighed and went to the window to stare out at the gusty morning and wondered what she could have done or said to make everything all right for Julie. But it was too late. Three years ago when George had discarded them both for someone he loved better, he had taken all Julie's faith and security with him.

Peggy had done all she could to restore that lost faith and had thought — had known — that Tom would do the rest. She hadn't realised that marriage for Julie would be the biggest hurdle of all.

She sighed again as a sudden handful of rain spattered against the window. Then she fetched Julie's umbrella and put it in a strategic position in the hall.

Julie would argue of course. She hated any sort of accoutrement, just as George had. Peggy remembered how he used to scheme his way out of shopping expeditions in case he had to carry parcels.

The small thought made her eyes fill with unexpected tears. She wanted to lean her head against the wall and whisper, "Oh, George . . ." But of course she didn't.

Then just as Julie was arguing fiercely about the umbrella, Tom arrived outside in his battered old car to take her to the office. Late for work himself, he was determined Julie shouldn't get wet.

Peggy forgot to be objective and pleaded in a whisper, "Please, darling, don't say anything you'll regret. He loves you so much . . ."

Julie simply stared. Her face was so raw with uncertainty that Peggy wanted to cry out.

She shut the door on the two of them and leaned against it. Then she said aloud, as if to an accuser, "There's nothing I can do about it. There's nothing I can do . . ."

IT was Peggy's mother-in-law who had first, unwittingly, revealed the depths of Julie's unhappiness.

Mrs Russell, Senior, always came on Christmas Eve and birthdays, armed with presents and concern and a kind of apologetic diffidence. Though she was genuinely fond of her mother-in-law, Peggy dreaded these visits.

Mrs Russell had said once, "You know, Peg, it's all over now between George and that woman. If only you could forgive him . . ."

"I don't want to talk about it, Mother." Peggy had said, and Mrs Russell's hand had whitened on her old-fashioned handbag.

But last Christmas Eve, Peggy had been pleased to see her. She'd known for some time that she would have to contact George about Julie's marriage and her mother-in-law would be the perfect messenger.

Mrs Russell had arrived in the evening with a twin-set for Julie and a frivolous underset for Peggy.

"You can change them if you don't care for the colour or anything," she said apologetically.

Julie had been her typically honest self about it. "Granny darling, I've heaps of sweaters and things. Could I possibly change it for a tablecloth and maybe some napkins?"

Mrs Russell had been only a second catching on.

"Julie! My dear," she cried delightedly. "Who is it and when? Have you anywhere to live?"

Julie had laughed and begun to extol Tom's manly virtues. Watching her, Peggy had regretted that she hadn't taken the trouble to tell Mrs Russell three months ago when Julie and Tom were first engaged. Obviously Julie felt no guilt at all about it. That was rather awful too, thought Peggy sadly.

To cover her own embarrassment she had said quickly, "Would you like to get Granny's present now, Julie?"

When Julie had left the room, Mrs Russell said fondly, "Isn't it marvellous that she's found Mr Right so soon, Peg?" Then she looked embarrassed.

Peggy had followed her line of thinking only too well and smiled briefly.

"Mother, I wonder whether you'd mention Julie's engagement the next time you see George? He'd probably like to write and tell her he's in favour of it or something."

"Yes, of course." Mrs Russell clasped her hands together on her old bag. "Wouldn't it be rather nice if Julie wrote to him herself? I mean . . . just to get in touch again . . ." Her voice tailed away.

"You mean she is still his daughter." Peggy heard her own voice as dry as dust. "I'll mention it. I don't suppose she will."

Mrs Russell sighed deeply and made the first ever criticism of her granddaughter.

"She is very unforgiving," she said.

Peggy answered with exaggerated calm. "He hurt her very much."

Mrs Russell's hands tightened.

"He hurt me, too," she said bravely. "But I still love him."

"Please. Mother. We shall only be upset."

"Is that bad? You haven't been upset for three years, but you don't look well on it."

Peggy was going to deny it, to say she had been upset every day of those three years. Then she couldn't. She had been bitter, but bitterness was a frozen emotion that had nothing upset about it.

Julie had come back then with the present. It was an electric blanket and Mrs Russell had been overwhelmed. She'd hugged them both and asked them over to tea on Boxing Day. Tom as well.

THEY had walked to Mrs Russell's bungalow on the outskirts of town, Julie and Tom hand in hand, swinging their arms and including Peggy in their bursts of laughter.

When they reached the raggle-taggle garden that would blossom into dense jungle in May, Tom was unexpectedly enchanted.

"I'm the same," he said when Julie explained that Granny could never bear to pull a weed. "I can never see why they shouldn't all have a chance." He looked fondly at Julie. "You must be very close to your grandmother."

Julie replied with her devastating honesty. "We hardly see her, do we, Mother? She's always trying to get us to kiss and make up with Father."

Tom looked at Peggy, but she couldn't meet his eyes.

"We're very fond of her," she excused them both lamely.

They walked up the narrow pathway in silence. The living-room was lamplit and the curtains were open. Julie tiptoed exaggeratedly through a frosty flower bed and peeped in.

Then her mouth thinned suddenly and she darted back.

"Father's there!" she hissed at Peggy. "Tom, what did I tell you? Just a put-up Christmas effort at getting the family together again."

Peggy knew that last year she would have felt the same anger. This year, she wasn't so sure.

"I expect he's spending Christmas here . . ." she began.

"Then why didn't Granny warn us?" Julie grabbed at her mother's arm and began propelling her back the way they'd come. "Let's go, quickly. They haven't seen us. It will be embarrassing if they look out of the window now."

Peggy felt herself pulling back. "Granny's expecting us, dear." And, she thought, Tom is with us, which would ease the situation. We could talk about the wedding and George could give his official blessing . . .

"I don't care. We must go, Mother." Julie looked almost desperate.

Tom spoke hesitantly in a strained voice. "Darling. I don't see what all the fuss is about. Your father is entitled to spend Christmas with his mother surely? And I do have to meet him some time."

Julie dropped her mother's arm and began to edge away. "Look, Tom, I know it's difficult to accept divorce, but it is a fact and you have to learn to live with it. If you weaken — just for an instant — it makes it twice as difficult."

Tom and Peggy looked at each other and then quickly away. Julie was already some way off.

Tom said diffidently, "I've put my foot in it. She's almost frightened of him. Surely she's seen him some time during the past three years? I mean, I thought legally he had access . . ." He was red with embarrassment. His own family were large and loving like he was himself.

Peggy tried to explain. "He came once or twice, but it was . . . difficult. You heard what Julie said . . ."

"She daren't let herself weaken," he murmured. "So she froze him out of her life." He looked torn in half. "She was just sixteen when she worked that out for herself. Come on, let's get back to the flat." He started running after Julie.

Peggy turned and stared at the lighted window, wondering if George knew they were expected, wondering if the last three years had aged him much, wondering if he fought off the spectre of loneliness each day as she had fought it, and failed.

Continued on page 107

The Sky's The LIMIT!

There I was with both feet firmly on the ground, chatting merrily to a pilot about the joys of gliding, says Eileen Elias. A few minutes later I was up there myself . . . at the controls!

by EILEEN ELIAS

EVER since I was a child I've always thought — how wonderful it would be to ride a bicycle in the sky! All that space, all that sunshine, and me sweeping and swooping, circling and gliding, with all my troubles and cares left behind.

Which was why, when someone recently offered me a seat in a car going down to watch a day's gliding, I accepted like a flash.

Gliding — now that surely would be the nearest thing to my celestial bicycle. Even if I wasn't up there myself, at least I'd be watching others do it.

"Don't get any ideas now," my husband said as I set off. "You know how much gliding costs an hour — or rather a minute?"

Astronomical. Yes, I knew. But watching didn't cost anything — and what a chance to go!

It was a glorious day as we motored down. I felt extra pleased because it was a Monday, too. Monday's usually washday, and I knew I ought to be doing other things.

But guilt only heightened my enjoyment. Let the wash take care of itself, I thought.

The gliding club certainly had "Welcome" on the mat for us. We told them we'd come to see the display.

Great, they said. But first we had a look round the clubhouse, and coffee. They showed us around, chatted us up in the cafeteria, and finally took the four of us outside on to the tarmac.

It was all I'd ever hoped for — fascinating to the last detail. Blue skies, and above us, tiny engineless gliders floating gently into space. It looked so easy.

I'd always wondered how a glider ever got off the ground. Well, now I saw for myself. Up came this great red tractor thing, hooked each saucy little glider on to its tail with a tow-rope, and — whoops! — they were away.

Borne upwards at speed, the gliders rose and rose into the sky, winched higher and higher by the tractor below, till next thing you knew the rope was paid off and the gliders, effortless as birds, were sailing above us.

We all watched, breathless. We must have watched for a full two hours before someone said, "What about a spot of lunch?"

Over the soup I voiced my admiration. Over the meat and two veg. our instructor hosts looked, I fancied, a tiny bit thoughtful. It wasn't till the sweet arrived that one of them caught the other's eye, nodded and spoke.

"Like to try, then?" he asked me.

"What, *me?*" I gasped.

"All of you, if you'd care to. Quarter of an hour each. What d'you say?"

It was the others who said it. I was speechless. But in seconds, it seemed, it was all arranged. We'd each have a go before we went home.

NOBODY else around me seemed to be having any qualms — they were all far too thrilled to be getting a quarter of an hour's gliding all free. I cursed myself for feeling scared, and followed our party out on to the tarmac.

The glorious morning had dulled a little, and now it was definitely chilly — or had I got cold feet?

As there was only one glider between us, someone had to be last up, and inevitably the someone was me. That meant an hour and a half of waiting around on the windswept tarmac, watching everybody else till my turn came. Somehow I didn't relish that.

I shuffled my feet around to keep warm, and turned up my coat collar. Every time one of them went up, my spirits went down — lower. The sky looked leaden. I thought of thunderstorms, and quailed. For two pins I'd have turned and ran.

"Well, here we are," said the cheery little instructor at my side. "Sorry you've had to hang about all this time, but just step this way."

He hoisted me up into the seat and buckled me in. Well, I was for it now, with no chance of escape. It wasn't till I had done up the last of the innumerable buckles that I grasped the frightful truth — my instructor wouldn't be sitting in front of me, comfortably protective. He'd be out of sight behind me.

All alone I was, with the controls before me, not knowing what to do, and about to be hurtled hundreds of feet into the air. Little comfort to know that someone was working dual controls if you couldn't even see him doing it. But there was no time to argue — we were off.

★ ★ ★ ★

There was the great tractor in front, pulling us along with a rush. Then whoof! Up we went.

There was no time to breathe. Now the whole contraption was shooting straight up into the air, taking my stomach with it. Now it was righting itself and we were airborne. I yelled behind me:

"What do I do?"

"Just keep a steady course," came the voice.

A steady course! I stared straight in front of me, not daring to look round or down. It was like being in the driver's seat of an enormous bus, pressed right up against the glass.

I felt anxiously about with my feet. There seemed to be some sort of pedal arrangment there below. Yes, pedal it was. It was really and truly a bicycle in the air! Just like my childhood dream — only now it was true and I was terrified.

"When you want to go left," said the voice behind me, "just pedal left. And right for right. Simple."

Simple! Well, maybe. My stomach had settled now, and I dared to take a swift glance downward. Immediately I wished I hadn't. Were those tiny roofs really houses, not a child's scattered toys? Those miniature farms and church steeples and minute crawling cars — were they really so far below?

I must have pedalled too hard with my left foot then, for suddenly the whole flying bicycle keeled over and swerved sickeningly sideways.

"Pedal right!" shouted the voice.

I pedalled frantically to the right, and over we tipped to the other side.

The sky spun round in a half-circle, and just missing a clump of trees and a pond, which rose out of nowhere, we swung back again. Thank heaven for somebody behind me who knew what we were at. I certainly didn't.

It was very quiet up here, I noticed for the first time. Deathly silent. No engine or anything to break the stillness. It was like flying into a vacuum, and I began to freeze to the controls. Would we go gliding on like this for ever?

The instructor's voice came over. "We're coming down now."

I STILL don't know which of us did it, he or I, but gradually we were circling lower.

My aerial bicycle lunged gently downwards, as though it was suffering a slow puncture. Green fields gave way to tarmac, and suddenly there they were — those little figures of our party, whom I thought I'd never see again. Real-life people walking towards us as the little glider slid to a halt.

"Great fun, wasn't it?" one of them said as I struggled with belts and buckles and stumbled out. My legs felt wobbly and my teeth were chattering.

"You all right?" said my instructor.

"Fine." I gasped. "It's turned a bit colder, hasn't it? But it was a wonderful trip."

Wonderful, I told myself, to be alive and on earth instead of up in the clouds. Wonderful to be me again, with home to go back to, and — yes, even the Monday wash.

As we sped homewards in the car, the sun came out again, and my companions looked up at the wide blue sky.

"Just think," said someone, "we've all been up there!"

But my dreams of coasting through space were over for ever. A bicycle on earth seemed infinitely more preferable, now, to a bicycle in the sky. ■

Continued from page 104

PEGGY watched the glow go out of Julie and Tom after that incident. They went ahead with their plans as before, they gloated over their fast-filling bottom drawer, they chattered and laughed often. Perhaps too often.

Occasionally Julie would throw her arms around Tom and hug him desperately as if they were parting on a railway station for ever.

And Tom would stroke her hair as if she were a child and then kiss her and say, "It's all right, my love." Then Julie would break away, laughing again.

The glacial February day they'd arrived together for tea, Julie had missed the postman that morning and Peggy had put the letters on the mantelpiece for her.

Tom and she had watched Julie read them, the firelight dancing on her dress and hair.

When she came to her father's writing Peggy knew she had recognised it immediately, but Julie paused only a moment before slitting the envelope and reading the contents.

"Acceptances," she said in a curiously artificial voice. "Aunt

Madge says can we put her up? Should be addressed to you, Mum, but there's all sorts of advice for young brides included, so I suppose she thought she'd better put my name on the envelope . . ."

There was an awkward silence before Peggy asked, "What did your father say?"

Tom was suddenly very still. Peggy thought compassionately: he's just as involved in this as we are.

Julie replied casually enough. "Just pleased about the good news. Wishes Tom and me all the best. Granny must have told him. You didn't write, did you?" She looked almost accusing.

Peggy shook her head. She wished she could have found the courage to write. This strain between Tom and Julie was not her doing, yet she knew she could not escape responsibility for it.

Tom said over-cheerfully, "That's jolly nice of him." He knew better than to suggest they call or write back now. Instead he changed the subject.

"Listen. I've got some news. Those houses we looked at on Riverside — I can get a mortgage. The first five years will be tough, but if we're staying there for the rest of our lives it will probably be just as economical as a flat."

Julie was hysterical with joy. "Tom, you angel!" Her face glowed. "Oh, darling, it will be wonderful! I'm certain we can manage it. Let's go into ways and means after tea."

Peggy watched Tom. He seemed content as always but he had an air of waiting for something. When Julie went upstairs, she asked him quietly whether he ought to go in for such an expensive home.

"You mean, am I just doing it to please Julie?" He grinned his attractive grin. "Oh, I know in a flat we could have afforded luxuries. Maybe a car. But Julie doesn't need things like that. This need of hers for a proper home goes deeper than furniture and food-mixers."

Peggy nodded. Sometimes it hurt to see how well Tom knew her daughter.

He went on, picking his words carefully. "I told her just now, after she'd had the letter from her father, because I suppose I hoped for something from her in return . . ."

Peggy said wearily, "Tom, it would be no good Julie going to see him, if that's what you're after. Over three years the two of us have built up this wall . . ."

Tom said stubbornly, "Forgiveness has to start somewhere."

NOW, on this gusty morning those words echoed in Peggy's head like an accusation. Forgiveness. Was that what was wanted from her? As an example to her daughter?

She tried to think rationally about George, to put herself in his place. She tried to understand the terrible infatuation that had made him leave his wife and daughter: the feelings of guilt he must have been left with, the consequent loneliness.

But how could she forgive him when she could never forget?

Somehow the long day passed until Julie came home. She looked tired. Peggy made coffee and built up the fire and told herself not to worry. But Julie knew.

"It's all right. Mum, the presents don't have to go back." She didn't smile and neither did Peggy. "I didn't talk to Tom after all. When it came to the point there seemed nothing to talk about."

Peggy bowed her head. "Darling, I was wondering. Would Tom feel better about it all, if your father came to the reception?"

Julie made a sharp negative gesture with her hand. She seemed to shudder with revulsion.

"He walked out and left us for another woman, Mother — remember? And if you're trying to look at it from his angle — and don't think I haven't tried to do that, too — it would hardly be pleasant for him to sit there and watch Uncle Fred give me away. And then listen to his speech about when I was a little girl and Cousin David ducked me in the river . . ."

"All right, darling." Unconsciously Peggy put her hands over her ears.

And yet as the wedding day came nearer, Peggy remembered again and again that George hadn't been invited and there was a strange ache in her heart. At last she went to see Mrs Russell.

She sat opposite her in the small cluttered bungalow and gripped her handbag just as her mother-in-law usually gripped hers. She didn't know what to say and they talked about the first crocuses poking up in the tangled garden outside and the awful windy weather.

At last she said, "Will you tell George, Mother, try to explain that — that Julie is overwrought at this time? Otherwise she would want him to come to the wedding reception. Naturally . . ." She heard her own voice, painfully embarrassed. ". . . of course he will see her in church."

Mrs Russell said quietly, "Here's his address, Peg. Can't you tell him yourself?"

"I'd prefer if you . . ." Peggy picked up the envelope, careful not to glance at the address.

Mrs Russell sighed. "He won't be at the church, Peg. He said it would upset you and Julie. But he might come if you went and asked him."

"No!" Peggy thrust the envelope into her pocket and stood up. "He might think I want him to . . ."

As Peggy walked down the rain-soaked path, she looked back and saw that her mother-in-law's eyes were wet with tears.

THE day of the wedding was sunny and blustery and the flat was bursting with relatives. They were all up early and about their various duties.

Uncle Fred practised his speech in the bathroom, Aunt Madge went to the hairdresser and Cousin David flirted with the bridesmaid in the dining-room. Peggy was alone with Julie in her bedroom. And Julie was crying.

"Darling, please don't worry." Peggy fetched a box of tissues. "It's only wedding nerves. Everyone suffers from them. I can remember . . ." She stopped quickly.

"Quite." Julie looked at her mother in the mirror. They were very alike. "It could happen to me one day. Just like you and father."

Julie slumped into her bedroom chair. Her lovely dress billowed around her. Sobs hiccoughed in her throat. The flood gates were opened at last and she could not stop talking.

"Tom said — he said if I couldn't forgive my father for what he had done, how could I ever forgive him if *he* did something stupid. Well, of course I said I couldn't. He just looked at me, Mother, as if I'd failed him in some way. What does he expect of me?"

"Tom would never leave you, darling," said Peggy placatingly. "You must trust him — he loves you."

"I had trust in Father, too. So did you. He loved us."

"Yes, but Tom doesn't mean that . . ." Suddenly Peggy couldn't be objective any longer. ". . . He means that once you cut off your love, even if it's an unwanted love, it makes you into a mean person. It stunts other love. It's not good for you." She knew she had got hold of the truth at last.

Julie said numbly, "I've tried to think about Father. Just think about him. But I can't any more. I hardly remember what he looks like."

Peggy stared at the tear-stained face and made up her mind quickly. Maybe it wasn't too late after all.

"You go on getting ready, Julie. I won't be long. I'll bring you some black coffee and you'll feel fine."

She used Uncle Fred's car and drove around the outskirts of town and across the river to the moors. Once, George and she had promised each other they would retire to a cottage there and spend their days watching the herons and telling the seasons by the skeins of wild geese flying overhead.

THE lanes seemed endless and the scattered cottages had their names tucked shyly behind laurel bushes and willow trees.

Eventually she came to a squat, grey stone labourer's cottage, one up and one down, with its front door planted firmly on the road's edge. The garden was small, carefully cultivated.

George was bending over, dropping potatoes into prepared holes. He straightened at the sound of the car and leaned on the fence. As Peggy got out in her neat wedding outfit, his face did not change, but his hands whitened on the fence.

"George." Peggy didn't know what to say. "George, I want to see you about . . ."

"Come on in, Peg." He wiped his hands on his trousers and opened the low front door. He hadn't changed much. He was older of course, there were lines on his face and his hair was greyer.

But he still had a way of bending his head before he spoke then suddenly lifting it and looking directly at her. "Will you have some coffee?"

She was terribly nervous. "There isn't time. I came — I came to see if you would . . . if you could possibly come to the wedding."

George stood resting his hands on the deal table which took up most of the floor space. Everything was heart-breakingly neat.

He lifted his head. "Mother told me. I thought it best to stay away."

"No, George. Come to the wedding. To the reception." She took a deep breath. "George, I want you to give Julie away."

He straightened then. "I thought Fred . . ."

"Fred's there, he said he'd do it. But I want you to give our daughter away." Tears ran down her face and on to her two-piece. "Please, George. Please."

She felt as if she had been made of ice and the ice was melting right away. She thought incredulously — you don't need to forget after all . . . you can still forgive . . .

He said in a low voice. "Peggy. My dear Peggy. Please don't cry."

She tried to explain about Julie and found she was explaining about herself. And he understood. That was the wonderful thing. He understood perfectly.

She went upstairs to lay out his clothes while he scrubbed at the sink. She looked out of the tiny bedroom window at the neat kitchen garden hemmed in by the empty moors, and she thought — it's begun. The forgiveness had to start somewhere. And it's starting here and now.

JULIE was still sitting on the bedroom chair when her father and mother came into her room. She stared at her father, as if she was trying to hate him just as she had done three years ago.

He stood with his back to the door and his head bowed, as if to receive her scorn, and then, suddenly, he straightened and stared at her.

He looked startled as if he had never seen a girl in a wedding dress before. Then he cleared his throat and said huskily, "I hope he's a better man than I am."

Peggy almost gasped at such complete honesty, such humility. And she realised suddenly that such honesty can lead into much deeper trouble than any amount of polite compromise.

Her husband could not live with two women as many men might have done. He had chosen the wrong one and lived with unhappiness ever since.

A slight movement from the chair drew Peggy's gaze from her husband to her daughter. And suddenly, she knew that Julie was ready to forgive, too. She had inherited her father's honesty, and recognised it in him.

Julie cleared her throat and said quietly, "Tom wanted to meet you."

Peggy knew that was the nearest Julie could come just then to a reconciliation, and she willed George to understand and accept it.

He smiled, a well-remembered smile. "Let's not disappoint him then."

Julie stood up very tall.

"He won't be disappointed," she said, "will he, Mother?"

*** THE END ***

MOTHER KNOWS BEST

All her life she'd believed that to be true, until the day her son taught her a very important lesson.

MARIE KELLY twisted a loose curl at the back of her fair head and looked tenderly at her older son before returning to the arithmetic lesson.

Multiplication tables. Would he ever learn them?

"Let's go over it once again, Allan. It just needs a little bit of practice."

Practice! It would take more than that, Marie thought. Her other son, Eric, knew them already without practising and he was a year and a half younger than Allan. And he could read better.

She sighed. He was also better at football, would never need braces on his teeth, didn't have to wear glasses, and he'd never had an asthma attack. And Allan . . . Where was the justice?

"You're tired, Mum. Maybe Dad'll help me. Or I can try it by myself."

She wished Allan hadn't sensed her fatigue. Why had she shown it? She had to try to build his confidence, to protect him from his brother's perfection, but studying at home was often a bore, and her guilt spun around her painfully.

"I'm not tired, Allan. Come on. We'll try it again."

Night after night. Where did he get his patience? If only Rob would relieve her with it. But he usually arrived home so exhausted that he'd sink into an armchair and spend the evening reading the newspaper, or watching television with Eric.

"Let the boy study alone, or let Eric help him." Rob always said the same thing.

She always answered the same way. "Don't you think it's humiliating enough for him as it is?"

"All right, Marie, forget Eric then. But let Allan try it alone. It'll do him good."

Complete Story by PATRICIA McCUNE IRVINE

That was the trouble with Rob. He didn't understand Allan's predicament. He never really had.

Marie remembered the day, two years before, when the situation had been thrown into sharp focus. Allan and Eric were taking their intermediate swimming tests at the public pool together, although Eric was barely six years old. But Marie knew he would make it easily.

As the two boys plunged in with the rest of the class to swim the length of the long pool, she kept her fingers crossed behind her back for Allan. Relax, Allan, she begged silently. Don't drag your legs. Don't bob your head. Kick your feet. You can make it.

The class splashed through the water, reckless but determined, losing identities in the turmoil. Then suddenly, in one sweeping motion, the swimming instructor lifted Eric from the churning pool.

"Out you go," he ordered. "That's as far as you're swimming today."

KINDLY COPPER

It was a special day for me when I rushed across a busy road and twisted my ankle, many years ago.

A handsome bobby who had been on point duty directing traffic came to my rescue.

We have now been married for thirty years and to this day he still calls me his "lucky pick-up."

It took Eric a moment to recover from the shock. Then he bellowed, "What do you mean? I'm not tired! I can swim the length of the pool, easily. Why did you pull me out?"

The instructor's voice was decisive and conclusive. "You were working too hard. You're not ready yet. You can try again next week."

"I am ready! I can do it!"

"The idea is to swim the length of the pool in an easy, relaxed manner. You were chopping your way like a toy boat in a bath. It's not good enough."

Marie had suddenly realised she was wringing her hands. Her mouth was open to speak but she could say nothing. Out of the corner of her eye she saw Allan reach the far end of the pool and something inside her gave a small voiceless "thank you" to the instructor.

But she knew Eric was the better swimmer of the two. Everyone knew it. Eric knew it. The instructor knew it. Then why . . . ?

"Eric could have made it easily," the instructor admitted to her when the boys were out of hearing distance. "After he swims it next week he'll forget all about the incident.

"But Allan will remember for a long time. It's important to him that he was first. He has more confidence already. It's difficult for him having a little brother who — well, you know how it is."

Yes, she knew how it was. She'd tell Rob what had happened, then maybe he'd understand. But Allan told him first.

"Dad, you should've seen me! I passed the swimming test on the first try. I'm ready to go into the advanced class."

Couldn't Rob see Allan was pleased? Couldn't he see how important this achievement was? A few more successes, and there was no telling what it might eventually lead to.

"But, Marie, do you honestly think that was fair to Eric?" Rob asked when they were alone and she'd explained the incident at the pool. "I mean if he could have done it — and we know he's a better swimmer than Allan — do you think it was the right thing for the instructor to do? In all fairness?"

His voice was higher pitched than usual and Marie closed her eyes for a moment, hoping the right words would come to her.

"Rob, can't you understand when you look at Allan? Can't you see what that one small experience has done for him? Eric's forgotten about it already, but Allan hasn't."

Marie knew she was just repeating the instructor's words, but she knew he was right, although Rob would never agree. That was always the trouble.

SO for almost two years she'd struggled on without Rob. It was the same week after week. Multiplication tables. Reading aloud. Eye exercises. Piano lessons.

It was the least she could do to build the boy's confidence. Teach him responsiblity. Make him a good, willing worker.

Only small successes broke through from time to time, but if Allan was not always perfect or correct or quick to answer, he was nevertheless a good boy, polite, patient.

He knows his shortcomings, Marie thought one Saturday while preparing dinner. Yes, he's a good boy.

She knew he'd never have Eric's handsomeness, or his outgoing personality, or his ability to make friends, or his quick mind, but well — he was a good boy. That was enough.

She felt a warm glow of well-being and stood quite still for a moment, just thinking about it. She turned at the sound of the back door opening.

It was Eric. Home from playing football for his school.

"You're late — oh, Eric."

He stood quietly inside the door, holding his limp right arm carefully with his left hand. He didn't say a word. Just big brown eyes, moist, pleading, and that broken arm.

It was three o'clock before they were able to leave the hospital. She sat in the back seat of the car with Eric and he fell asleep in her arms before they were halfway home.

He stayed close to her on Sunday and she helped him dress and fed him his breakfast.

"Mummy, read me a story," he demanded in the early afternoon. Marie remembered he hadn't called her Mummy for several years and he'd never wanted her to read to him. "I'll read it myself," he'd always said.

And now: "Read me a story, please."

"All right, Eric. I'll read to you."

He's like a baby, she thought, wondering what strange request would come next. All because of a broken arm. A broken arm. The meaning puzzled her and she read mechanically, trying to understand.

"You don't want to read to me, do you?" Eric's eyes seemed to accuse and then they revealed a pain she'd never seen before.

"Why, Eric, of course I do." She took his chin in her hands and looked into his eyes. "What made you say that?"

"You don't really sound interested. You seem to be thinking about something else. Mum, would you let me say the multiplication tables to you? Will you time me? Just see how quickly I can do them."

Multiplication tables!

MARIE felt the pounding inside her, the terrible lightness in her head and the heaviness around her heart. What in heaven's name had she done to Eric?

"Of course I'll listen to your tables, Eric. Let me hear you."

She timed him as he recited them, and she timed him a second time so he could beat his record. Then he wrote his name for her with his left hand, and she wrote for him with her left hand. And when she tried to leave him he wouldn't let her go.

"I have a broken arm," he said, "so now I'm as important as Allan."

I have a broken arm, so now I'm as important as Allan.

The words hit her so hard they brought a cry from the depths of her throat. She dropped to her knees and put both arms around him and drew him close, so he couldn't see her eyes.

"Eric . . ." What could she say to him? What could a mother say to a son she'd — she'd neglected? "Eric, I . . ."

"You're crying, Mum. Why are you crying?"

"Because I have to tell you something, Eric." Oh, it was all clear now. "But you might not understand it or even believe me."

"I'll believe you, Mum."

She knew he wanted to. But telling him that she loved him wouldn't be good enough. She'd have to show him, prove to him, make him believe in his heart.

What Would We Do Without Them?

A FRIEND of mine who has just moved into a new house was telling me the other day about one of her neighbours.

"She's an amazing person," she said. "No matter when you meet her she always seems to be cheerful and chatty. She has really helped me settle in so easily."

I knew exactly what she meant. We've all met people like my friend's new neighbour from time to time — people who, with their sheer optimism and cheerfulness, can make what could have been a trying experience a rewarding one.

We've all set out on a long, boring train journey and seen a compartment of silent strangers brought to life by someone who just refuses to go along with the famous "British reserve."

Only a few days ago I had the good fortune to see it happen again — this time in a dentist's waiting-room.

For ten minutes I'd sat there with half a dozen or so other women in a tense silence.

There wasn't much to look at and all our eyes were fixed on a toy the dentist had installed to amuse his younger patients.

It was a duck, large enough to take a child on its back, and it was set on a strong spring.

The movement of people coming and going kept it in a perpetual rocking motion and there we all sat, pale and unsmiling, staring at it.

Then the door opened and a youth of about eighteen breezed in.

He sat down, looked round at us all, then at the bobbing duck.

"All right, own up," he said unexpectedly, "which one of you ladies was having a go on the duck before I came in?"

There was a second's silence, then we all exploded into laughter.

Like magic the atmosphere changed and we all began to talk.

He didn't make me — a self-confessed coward when it came to dentists — enjoy my appointment exactly. But he certainly made it a lot easier.

As important as Allan. So in his own way, Rob had been right all along.

"Eric, pick out another story. I'll read it to you in a minute, just as soon as I get back. First, I have something important to tell your father."

Something very important.

*** THE END ***

"Wee Sleekit Cowrin' Tim'rous Beastie"

That's what Robert Burns said about a mouse. In our case the description applied more to Dad — who had to do battle with the invader!

By LEN FOX

ONE evening I returned home after taking our thoroughbred mongrel for his evening excursion around the cemetery at the back of the house. I was immediately confronted at the kitchen door by our three children leaping frenziedly about and shouting something about a monster being in the house.

"A real monster!" my eldest son Paul said in a grim whisper.

"Where?" I asked cautiously.

"In the bathroom," came the chorused reply.

"And, er, how . . ." I ventured tentatively. "How big is it?"

Paul spread wide his hands.

My heart began to pound. What

weapons would I need? A poker, yes, how about a poker?

No, that's no good, we've got a gas fire. High speed, natural, pokerless gas.

How about the dog? Send the dog in — alone!

I looked at Digger sitting there, tongue lolling, waiting with pleading eyes for his customary drink of water.

Send the dog in? I had to be joking!

Then I noticed Paul's hands had begun to move, and that the gap between them was closing slowly, until his index fingers were a mere two or three inches apart.

I slumped with relief. Our monster turned out to be a mouse.

I went into the living-room and sat down in the fireside chair to plan my next move.

Six years as a cemetery worker had given me a fondness for nature, an aversion to the unnecessary killing of any creature and a shelf in my bookcase half-filled with those small, slim volumes much beloved by schoolboys and amateur naturalists.

Each book had been purchased on the spur of the moment as I discovered something of interest in the country. And each was read avidly for two or three days, then placed proudly in the bookcase — to remain untouched for months on end.

"Paul, hand me that book on wild animals," I said decidedly.

I knew that field mice sometimes sought the shelter of a handy house. After a week of heavy rain surely it was quite likely that a field mouse would seek refuge from the soggy cemetery?

If this were the case my trusty animal book would give me the information I needed regarding its habits and thus enable me to trap it alive.

THE Long-Tailed Field Mouse," I read, "is about three-and-a-half inches long . . ."

My courage was returning fast.

"It's timid, gentle in disposition and short-sighted."

My confidence soared.

". . . Food — grain, nuts, fruit . . ."

I stopped reading. Grain, nuts, fruit? That sounded strangely familiar.

A moment's thought and it came to me. I went to the kitchen cupboard, and there it was — a packet of that Swiss-style breakfast cereal. Perfect field mouse bait.

I got an empty wide-necked milk bottle from the kitchen and poured in a spoonful of the cereal, making sure a little stuck to the rim as an extra enticement.

Then I set off up the stairs to begin my "wild mouse" hunt.

There was a small scuffling sound at the far end of the landing and I hesitated.

"Timid, gentle, short-sighted," I reminded myself.

I reached the open bathroom door just in time to see a tiny brownish mouse scuttle quickly away into a hole where the washbasin pipes ran along the floor and through the hardboard panelling of the bath.

Placing the milk bottle on the floor with the neck towards the hole, I squatted on my heels and waited.

And waited — and waited . . .

Suddenly the mouse scampered from the hole, stopped, did a quick circle of the bathroom floor, scrambled over my foot and went back into the hole.

I straightened up as quietly as I could, cursed the "pins and needles" in my foot, and all the time kept my eyes on the hole.

A small head appeared. Timidly the mouse tasted the cereal on the neck of the bottle, did a little dance of joy and dashed back out of reach.

I squatted down again, hand poised.

"Next time, Mr Mouse, next time," I muttered.

Suddenly there was a scuffling and squeaking and *two* mice shot from the hole, one pursuing the other around the bathroom floor. The smaller of the two finally fled through the bathroom door, and the other returned to its hiding place.

I was stunned!

Two mice! I hadn't planned for that, and realised dejectedly that I'd never get them in the bottle together!

As I squatted there pondering the problem, the smaller mouse returned. It glided across the bathroom floor, entered the bottle and commenced chewing.

So the book was right after all. I had a short-sighted mouse!

My hand swooped down and grasped the bottle. I had a brief glimpse of the second mouse dashing in and out of the bottle neck as I swung the bottle upright.

I CARRIED my furry little prisoner downstairs to receive the acclamation of the children. They, however, showed great concern for the mouse and a complete lack of interest in the method of capture.

Somewhat dispirited, I collected and prepared a second milk bottle. Naturally the trap wouldn't work again but I had to try.

For a full thirty minutes I squatted ridiculously between washbasin and bath, eyes straining in the gathering dusk. But after that thirty minutes I was the proud possessor of a second imprisoned mouse.

Watching the two bottled mice nibbling their breakfast cereal, I began to make plans to rear them as family pets. But my plans were shattered by the sudden arrival of my wife. Her words on the matter were few, but choice and to the point.

Sadly, I carried my two prisoners out into the middle of the darkened cemetery and set them free.

The following day there was a field mouse in the yard. It wasn't the same one of course. I mean, it couldn't be — could it . . . ?■

WHO WANTS A CUBE?

In a London restaurant recently I sat at the same table as an American lady.

Before she left, she took two or three lumps of sugar with the restaurant's name on the wrappers.

I must have looked at her suspiciously for she stopped in her tracks and smiled.

"Wherever I go I take wrapped sugar for souvenirs," she explained. "I put them in a large bowl on my coffee table. They're a fascinating talking point with my guests, as they have different names from all over the world."

Every day he caught the same train to work. Then one morning he found himself wondering if he really knew where he was going . . .

All The Grey Daddies

Complete Story
by EILEEN ELIAS

GEOFF GODDARD reached into the back seat for his briefcase and raincoat, as his wife slowed the car to a halt outside the station. It wasn't always easy to find a place to park, even for a few minutes, at this time of the morning.

He kissed Mary briefly on the cheek and scrambled out into the pale morning sunshine.

"Daddy!" Simon's voice was plaintive as he squirmed in his seat in the back. "You didn't say what you always say!"

"Sorry." Geoff paused with his hand on the door. "'Bye-Simon-be-a-good-boy-and-look-after-your-mother."

Simon's round face relaxed in a satisfied beam. Geoff could never get away without the same morning ritual. He gave Simon a playful poke in the ribs and turned again to Mary. "Anything I've forgotten?"

Mary pushed back her hair and smiled. Her hair was soft and fine, and fell over her forehead just as it had done the first day he met her — when was it, six years ago?

Watching the familiar gesture, Geoff felt a momentary surge of pride. She looked ridiculously young amongst all the other wives taking their husbands to catch the 8.29 train.

"Well, yes," Mary was saying, "as a matter of fact there is. But it doesn't really matter."

"Tell me," Geoff demanded. "Quick, I'll have to dash. It isn't anybody's birthday, and it isn't our anniversary, so what've I forgotten?"

"Only that Roland's taking me to lunch," Mary said.

"And I'm staying at play school for dinner, Daddy!" Simon's triumphant shout from the back showed that he, at any rate, hadn't forgotten.

"Is that today?" asked Geoff. "It went clean out of my head."

Mary laughed. "There was no reason why you should remember. It's my date, not yours, but well, I'm looking forward to it. It'll be so nice to have a proper meal out at the Crown for once, instead of baked beans with Simon in the kitchen!

"Better get going, darling. Or you won't be one of Simon's grey daddies at all this morning!"

With a quick wave, Geoff joined the stream of commuters surging into the station.

Simon's grey daddies! It was a private joke between the three of them, the sort of family joke that nobody else could quite share.

Grey daddies. That's just what we all are, he thought. A stream of men in grey coats and suits, the uniform of City men, hurrying to their offices. Rushing to catch the 8.29 every morning and hurrying home again on the 5.47.

Yes, Geoff told himself, as he showed his ticket and hurried over the bridge, to a little boy of four, that would be just how they looked. Dozens and dozens of husbands and fathers leaving wives and children, to go their separate ways.

Simon to play school, himself to his drawing board at his office of consulting engineers, and Mary . . .?

Funny how he'd forgotten Mary's date, Geoff thought, as he waited on the platform. Roland had phoned her last week, out of the blue, to tell her he'd be down their way on a business trip, and would she like to have lunch.

Mary had been thrilled. A break like this in her daily routine was rare, she'd said. She'd accepted the surprise invitation at once.

When Geoff was at the office, he often thought of Mary, and what she was doing. Mary, in an apron, doing the morning's chores. Mary, chatting with friends at the shops; fetching Simon from play school, sitting down after their lunch together to watch TV.

Mary, in the garden, her soft hair bright in the sunshine. And then, at the end of the day, the drive to the station to collect him from the train, rather tired and hungry and ready for home.

But today would be different. Today she'd be lunching at the Crown — with Roland.

THE train drew in and Geoff surged forward with the rest. He was first into the carriage and settled down in a window seat. A few moments later the train pulled out.

"Phew. I only just made it this morning." It was Stevenson from along the road, red-faced and hanging on to a strap. "How do you always manage to get a seat?"

Geoff grinned. "I suppose I'm lucky. My wife drops me in the car.

"I know," Stevenson nodded. "I saw her just moving off." He squeezed in beside Geoff as somebody moved over. "Was that your boy in the back? Lively-looking kiddie."

"Mary takes him on to morning play school after she's dropped me," Geoff explained. "Nursery schools are great. Simon would stay at his all day if he could. He thinks it's a treat to have dinner there. He's staying today, as a matter of fact. My wife's got a lunch date."

Stevenson was nodding. "It does them good sometimes, these ladies' luncheon parties. Gets them out a bit. It must be dull, stuck in the house all day with nowhere to go."

He settled down with his paper, and Geoff, watching the endless houses flashing by, was left to contemplate what Stevenson had said.

A ladies' luncheon party. He wished it was. But Mary would be with Roland. Lunch with Roland at the Crown. Well — why not? Geoff asked himself furiously.

He'd heard all about Roland long ago — Mary had mentioned him shortly after they'd met. She and Roland had gone to school together, gone about in the same teenage crowd. Friends — well, again, why not? They had all of them been friends.

Roland had been at their wedding. Geoff could see him now, taller than himself, and darker. A confirmed bachelor — at least, he was twenty-seven and showed no signs of marrying.

Too busy, Geoff guessed. Roland was always busy. Those business trips of his were as sudden, surprising, dynamic as Roland himself. He'd always been the type to make money, do things in style.

There had been a time, once, just before he and Mary were married, when Geoff had felt more than a little envious of him. When the three of them had been out together, it had always been Roland with the money to spend.

Now, all these years after, it was still the same. Roland paid them flying visits from time to time, and they *were* flying visits, in every sense. He was for ever dashing off by plane somewhere, or just returning from somewhere else — business in Luxembourg, property deals in Spain.

The train jolted to a standstill, and suddenly it was all noise and crush. Geoff jumped to his feet, and jostled his way to the door. Stevenson was already out on the platform before him.

"Be seeing you," Stevenson said, swinging away into the crowd. "Have a good day."

"Thanks." Geoff followed him down the length of the platform behind all the other broad shoulders and shuffling feet. He smiled a little wryly. Simon's grey daddies! No Rolands among this lot.

GEOFF'S morning passed in a rush. Around eleven he snatched a moment for the coffee that Gillian the office junior brought to his drawing board.

For lunch Geoff sent out for a sandwich. He still had a lot of work to do and it didn't seem worth fighting through the crowds just for something to eat. Besides, he wasn't hungry.

He balanced the sandwich plate on his knee and glanced at the clock. Twenty past one. They'd be at the Crown now, in the blue and gold restaurant . . .

LOOK ON THE BRIGHT SIDE

A few weeks ago, I decided to go shopping to a nearby town. It was a lovely day, so I wore my sunglasses.

After parking the car, I passed a gift shop run by a charity and saw a beautiful embroidered belt in the window. I went into the shop, bought the belt and went on my way.

I later realised I had left my sunglasses at the shop. But when I returned to collect them, I was amazed to see them for sale in the window!

The lady in the shop thought I had left them on purpose as a donation!

He'd never been beyond the bar himself, but from there you could see the dark-blue carpet and little gold chairs. Mary would be sitting back in one of these, studying the menu.

Geoff pushed the sandwich plate away and crossed to the window. Mary was only having lunch with Roland. Why shouldn't she, if she wanted to?

Midday sun glistened on the leaves of the plane trees below in the square, and suddenly, irrationally, there was every reason in the world why not.

Because it was Roland, because it wasn't himself, because it would *never* be himself.

Never, if he worked till he dropped, would he make the sort of money that Roland could throw about on lunches at places like the Crown.

Never would he stop worrying inwardly about things like bills and wine lists and waiters when they went out for a meal.

Never would he go off casually by plane to Luxembourg or Spain to clinch business deals, always knowing that he was right.

People like Roland — they were born right, and they were right all through their lives. That's why they got on, made a success of things, did what they wanted. Instead of going up to town every day on the train, doing a dull job, going home again. Simon's grey daddies on the 5.47 . . .

"Are you OK, Mr Goddard?" Gillian, back from lunch, looked in from the door. "You only had a sandwich."

"I'm fine," Geoff said, turning from the sparkling green leaves of the plane trees.

"It would do you good to get out in the air, Mr Goddard. Even for ten minutes," Gillian said brightly. "Cooped up here all day. It does everybody good to have a change."

She disappeared back to the typists' pool.

Does everybody good. Geoff bent over his drawing board again. Would it do Mary good to have a change? A change, from somebody plodding, dull, unexciting, to someone forceful, someone going places?

He glanced at the clock on the wall. Only ten to two? Three and a half hours more. The afternoon couldn't pass quickly enough.

THE 5.47 was at the terminus two minutes early. Geoff was already waiting on the platform with the home-bound crowds, raincoat slung over his arm, case clutched nervously in his hand.

Out of the corner of his eye he saw Stevenson's bulky figure further down the platform. Purposely he pushed his way to another carriage. He didn't want Stevenson's remarks just now.

Finding a seat, he dropped into it with a sigh, and took the evening paper out of his case. The print swam before him. He closed his eyes, and felt the rocking of the train, gathering speed.

Home, home, home, soon he'd be home. And then?

Geoff automatically glanced at his watch as the familiar platform drew into sight. They were dead on time tonight. He pushed his way out, and walked past the booking office, out from the gloom of the station into the late evening sunlight.

There was the car, and Mary at the wheel. She stretched over to open the door as he reached the kerbside.

"Hello, dear. Had a good day?" She smiled.

Geoff didn't answer. He dropped into the passenger seat and stared straight ahead of him, avoiding Mary's face.

Simon's voice came shrilly from the back. "Daddy! You haven't said what you always say!"

Geoff made an effort. "Sorry. Hello-Simon-been-a-good-boy-and-looked-after-your-mother?"

Simon bounced up and down in his seat. "Yes, Daddy! Daddy, I stayed to dinner and we had shepherd's pie, and I ate up all mine.

When Mummy came for me in the car I looked after her all the way home!"

"Good lad." Geoff turned at last to Mary. "How did the lunch go?"

"Fine," she said. "It's nice at the Crown, Geoff. We had Chicken Maryland and tutti-frutti ice-cream."

Geoff watched Mary as she drove through the familiar streets, but the calm profile gave nothing away. She took a hand suddenly from the wheel and pushed back her hair. Recognising the gesture, Geoff felt comforted.

"How was Roland?" he made himself ask in a calm voice.

"Just like he always is. He never changes, does he?" Mary laughed. "Oh, by the way, he was sorry he couldn't stay to see you. He said he was all tied up for the rest of the day and his plane was leaving at six."

Geoff managed a smile. "He sounds exactly the same." He watched the little houses spinning past. "A get-up-and-go sort of chap, Roland," he said awkwardly. "I suppose you'd call him a successful man. I wish I had his pace."

"I'm glad you haven't," Mary said.

Geoff shot her a narrow glance. "Why?"

"You wouldn't have time for us," Mary turned the car into the driveway.

"Daddy!" Simon was bouncing on the back seat. "There's Ranger out in the next-door garden. Can I play with him before tea?"

Geoff saw the big dog poking his nose through the hedge, and reached over to let Simon out. The child went racing up the garden path, calling to Ranger. Mary opened her door, but Geoff put his hand on her arm.

"Wait a minute," he said quietly.

She looked at him, wondering.

"Mary. I'm never likely to get where Roland's getting. I tell myself I shall, but —" Geoff met her eyes. "Mary — it's true what Simon calls us. All the grey daddies. Dozens and dozens of us, streaming up to the station every morning, streaming back every night. It'll be like that for ever with me. Do you mind? Do you ever wish . . .?"

Mary half turned from the wheel, and touched his cheek with her finger. "Know something, Geoff? Simon's grey daddies. I never see them."

"What do you mean, never see them?" he asked.

Mary smiled. "Just what I say. All those people streaming out of the station, like they did tonight. I know they're there, but when I'm waiting in the car I don't see any of them.

"There's only one person, only one face I see. It comes out of the crowd, the same time every night and it's all I want, all I'll ever want. You — your face, darling."

*** THE END ***

Engaging Ways

Of all the romantic traditions, the giving of engagement rings must be the most precious, says Joan Biggar. At any rate, it's certainly one of the most popular in our history!

By JOAN BIGGAR.

IN the spring, a young man's fancy turns to thoughts of love — and a young woman's to engagement rings. And by early summer jewellers find that business has really warmed up from customers who come shopping two by two!

There are lucky days for getting engaged, too. In bygone times, Saturday and Sunday were the favourites, and according to the old wives, couples who became engaged at the weekend had the best chance of living happily ever after.

Mondays and Wednesdays are fortunate, too. Wednesday foretold a short engagement. Thursday — quarrels and possibly a change of heart, and Friday was thought downright unlucky for any new ventures, engagements included!

In the sixteenth century, young gallants, having chosen an appropriate day, took their sweethearts shopping for a "posy" ring. This was the very first "pledge of marriage" to be sold.

Posy rings were plain gold or silver

bands, but even more valuable to the wearer was the romantic message engraved inside, with the intertwined initials of herself and her loved one, and the date of their engagement.

Typical of the "posies" were couplets: "Wrong not the heart whose joy thou art," and "Thine own sweetheart, till death us part," in which the word "heart" was always replaced by a tiny engraving of a heart.

In Elizabethan times "gemmel" rings came into fashion. These were made up of two links which joined together when the ring was slipped on. Some were made in a design of a pair of mini hands clasping a heart, and the hands slid into contact as the double links closed on the "gemmel" or hinge.

Appropriate and charming though such rings were, however, by 1800 engagement rings were jewelled, like those of today, and the romantic message was no longer engraved, but spelt out in the gems.

A dazzling, rainbow ring was made up of Diamond, Emerald, Amethyst, Ruby, Emerald, Sapphire and Topaz, in that order, and if you put together the capital letters you get the posy "Dearest." A very pretty notion which must have cost some ardent suitor a pretty penny.

These days jewellers find the most popular gems for engagement rings are the diamond and sapphire, with the ruby in third place. And the best-selling designs are the diamond solitaire, with the large sapphire set between small diamonds, and the diamond and sapphire cluster.

Emeralds are scarce, and consequently the most precious jewels of all, but the lovely green tourmaline, though seldom requested, is the perfect choice for the girl with a sallow or olive skin.

However, not only the colour of the skin, but the shape of the hand must be taken into account when choosing the ring.

Square hands can flaunt a half hoop of jewels. Small dimpled hands seem made for a cluster or flower design in diamonds and sapphires, but also suit a solitaire, whilst the larger hand looks elegant wearing an oval ring, such as the popular oval sapphire set in a border of tiny diamonds.

The sapphire also makes a reddish hand appear whiter. Long, slim fingers make almost any ring look well, but particularly the oval, round and cluster shapes.

Traditionally the emerald is the jewel for redheads, sapphires are for blondes, rubies for brunettes, and nobody refuses diamonds!

THERE'S an old superstition that a vein runs straight from the third finger of the left hand to the heart, but really the engagement ring has always been worn on this finger for a more practical reason.

You see, placed here, the ring doesn't get knocked, as this finger can't be extended on its own, but only with the fingers on either side, so it's always well protected.

Now to some facts and fancies about the most precious stones for true lovers, the diamond, sapphire and ruby.

The diamond is the most durable of jewels, 85 per cent. harder than any other.

Generals often had diamonds set in their sword hilts, to bring them good fortune, and as a charm believed to protect them during battles.

Our present Queen, Elizabeth II, chose an all-diamond engagement ring, and although her predecessor Elizabeth I was never betrothed, she wore a diamond ring as a talisman to protect her against witchcraft and plague. Her cousin, Mary, Queen of Scots, had a wedding ring set with a rich diamond.

Virtue, purity, repentance, innocence and courage are just a few of the many traditional meanings given to this stone.

The third finger of the left hand is known as the finger of Apollo, and the deep blue sapphire is called Apollo's stone. Therefore, it is a natural choice for engagement rings.

The sapphire was regarded as a sacred stone by the Greeks, who worshipped Apollo, and, just as the diamond was the stone of the soldier, the sapphire was the gem of scholars. It was believed to encourage deep thought, and improve both the sight and the memory.

During this century the sapphire has been patronised by Royalty. It was the late Queen Mary's favourite jewel. And among the Royal ladies who have chosen sapphires for their engagement rings are the Queen Mother, the Duchess of Gloucester, the former and present Duchesses of Kent, Princess Alexandra, and Princess Anne.

The sapphire's traditional meaning is devotion.

Princess Margaret broke with Royal tradition by selecting her birthstone, the ruby, for her engagement ring. The ruby was once a great favourite, especially with the Victorians, who loved the colour, and it was supposed to combat evil by inspiring friendship and love.

So the "posy" for a ruby ring was often the Latin inscription "Omnia vincit amor" meaning "Love conquers all."

Jewellers find that most men spend lavishly when shopping for an engagement ring, spending as much, and sometimes more, than they can afford. Often this is wise, for jewellery increases in value as the spending power of money lessons, but few people look upon the engagement ring as a good investment!

Its value is sentimental, whatever it may have cost, and probably there is no other gift of which it is more true to say that, "It's the thought that counts." ■

Oh, These Weather Experts!

IT'S often been said that if we British didn't chat about the weather to each other, we'd go around all day and every day in silence!

It is certainly the case that most of us do discuss the weather with someone at least once a day.

My friend Sylvia talks about the weather any time, any place, to anybody who cares to ask her. You see, she was once in "the Met Offices" of RAF Bomber Command, and when she looks up at a sky, she doesn't see mere clouds such as you and I might.

She sees cloud formations of cirrus this and nimbus that!

Show her a weather map of the Atlantic, liberally sprinkled with low depressions here and there, and with an odd high pressure area somewhere around, throw in a few isobars and wind figures, and Sylvia will study it ecstatically.

"Ah!" she'll say happily. "How very interesting! I'm afraid we're going to have a very wet weekend!"

Now she had been known to be wrong. But *never* on "wet weekend" forecasts. If she says it will rain, you can depend on a near monsoon!

As her husband golfs with The Man Of The House at weekends, Sylvia is not, I'm afraid, top of the popularity polls for such gloomy but accurate forecasting.

Yet every week, around Wednesday or Thursday, two hopeful men ask once again: "What's the weather going to be like this weekend?"

Gluttons for punishment! But then aren't most fanatical golfers?

"THE MAN FOR ME"

Like most girls she had her romantic dreams. And dear, dull David everyone expected her to marry, featured in none of them . . .

I HAVE always lived in our little fishing village of Swn-y-Gwylan, which, before the commercial hotels were built, had a local population of less than five hundred. Swn-y-Gwylan is a romantic place — its Welsh name means "Sound of the Seagull" — but it's a proud place, too, naturally wary of outsiders.

When I was a girl I remember a wandering salesman in a startling turban and dark beard knocking on our door and opening a big case full of Eastern treasures. My mother was stern and suspicious.

"Not today, thank you!" she said and closed the door before the swarthy gentleman had time to say anything.

I felt sorry for the silk salesman. I was always one for giving people a hearing, especially strangers, which made my mother cross.

Only once did Mother melt when a visitor came to the door, but that was David Hopkins the fisherman's son, and you couldn't really call him a visitor, as he was born in Swn-y-Gwylan, too.

David Hopkins eased himself as painlessly as spring sunshine into our white-washed cottage by the harbour. My mother took to him like a cormorant to the waves. My father liked him, too, probably because of his soft voice and studious face.

Complete Story by MALCOLM WILLIAMS

"There's a gentleman for you, Rhianon," he constantly used to remind me. "Not like these fly-by-nights you see around the village these days!"

He was referring to the motor cyclists who roared into the sleepy calm of Swn-y-Gwylan in the summer, and the waiters and the barmen at the new hotels on the steep access road leading to the harbour.

My father used to work in the slate quarry behind the village once, but the quarry was gutted now, just an ugly shell that was worked out, a danger and a nuisance.

My father was partially crippled by an old accident in the quarry.

He'd worked afterwards as a slate dresser and could split slate as expertly as Mother could undo the layers of an onion. But nowadays he contented himself working in the chandler's shop, near the jetty, watching the lobster fishermen coming and going or mending their pots.

I came late into my parents' lives, so there never were young voices around me, except for David's, and our friendship grew naturally, and it pleased my parents. Mostly we went walking together, along the cliffs, enjoying the symphony of sand and surf and seagulls.

We watched the cormorants scouting the dark waves and the porpoises playing just beyond the harbour wall. We sang duets at home round our little piano with Mother rocking and knitting and Dad smoking his pipe. It seemed inevitable that one day we would be married.

David was scheduled to go to Lampeter College to train as a clergyman. I worked in the diminutive council building in the village, looking after agendas and taking minutes at meetings.

David and I, in the years of our courtship, never had a single crisis — until Colin Wilkes came to Swn-y-Gwylan.

COLIN was an outsider. Not only outside Cardiganshire, he wasn't even Welsh! As soon as Mother saw me take an interest in him she frosted up.

"I'd like to bring a new friend home for tea," I suggested hesitantly one day.

"If it's that . . . creature I saw you with after church last Sunday, definitely no!"

There was no arguing with Mother. Once her mind was made up she wouldn't budge. Her lips came together in disapproval, and her eyes challenged me.

"I haven't seen you much with David lately, Rhianon," my father added, supporting her. "I hope you haven't been playing hard to get."

"Oh, David!" I expostulated. "David's dead set on his career. He'll go away to Lampeter and I'll never see him again."

I walked out of the cottage in a fine tizzy and wandered round the harbour wall knowing that David made me so mad because . . . because he seemed to accept everything as inevitable.

He never did a thing to display his love for me. He just took me for granted, always had done. He'd never had to fight or suffer for me.

We'd been brought together by our parents' approval, and oddly, this had always made me a little rebellious and critical. There was fondness, and respect and liking but . . . something was lacking.

As I stood on the harbour wall with the wind whipping my hair and the seagulls mewing above me, I thought about Colin and wished he were with me now.

He worked as a waiter in the biggest hotel in Swn-y-Gwylan — and he rode a motorbike.

We'd met at a Saturday dance in the parish hall. The place had been packed, mostly with summer tourists, and the din had been deafening, causing the local councillors to raise a formal protest at the next committee meeting.

"We can't allow the tranquillity of Swn-y-Gwylan to be upset by hordes of rowdy visitors," had been the general comment. Although it wasn't my place, I'd spoken up, indignation lending me courage.

"If you want to take people's money hand over fist you must expect a bit of inconvenience now and then!"

Eyes had impaled me. It was a disloyal outburst, and I'd been coolly reprimanded afterwards but I didn't care.

Colin was like a breath of fresh air to me. He was a student from London and had got the hotel job by answering a newspaper advertisement.

I began avoiding David and instead of seaside walks I went off with Colin on his motorbike, sometimes as far as Aberystwyth to a dance. I thought of David going quietly off to be a preacher and suddenly it seemed I was living the right sort of life.

Over the next few weeks I bought some new, trendier clothes and had my hair styled.

Anyway, David didn't care. He seemed more concerned about reading books and making intense cultural conversations than wooing me. Colin was exciting, unpredictable and reckless.

Mother and Dad grew very anxious and I became the centre of disapproval.

"What on earth's got into you, child?" my mother constantly asked in exasperation. "You're not doing yourself justice with someone like that. Mark my words, if you play with fire you'll burn your fingers."

I couldn't see that. But I did know that with David the long years of invariable security had bored me. Anyway, he didn't care. He stopped calling at the cottage, and I put him out of my mind.

ONE Friday I was typing a report in the council office when the doorbell jingled and David came in. He looked nervous and worried.

"I didn't want to speak to you at the house, Rhianon? It's not fair to see you there," he explained.

"Oh, why's that?" I asked cautiously.

"Well . . . with your mam and dad there it's . . . inhibiting. You know what I mean?"

I raised my eyebrows.

"I would have thought you were on safe ground there," I said shortly.

David raked his slim fingers through his untidy hair. He wasn't good at small talk and he knew it.

"I wonder, Rhianon . . . if we could meet somewhere today?" The question hung in the air and I looked up into David's eyes.

My boss, Mr Clegg, blustered in then, wanting his typing in a hurry.

"I'll have it finished in two minutes, Mr Clegg. Then I'll bring it in to you," I promised.

Mr Clegg nodded, glanced anxiously at his watch, gave David a hostile stare and went back to his office.

"I'm sorry, David, I'll have to finish this now," I said quietly. He didn't reply. He looked intense and stiff.

"Would you take a walk with me lunch-time, Rhianon? I must talk to you."

I thought of the sandwiches, the Welsh cakes and the flask in my basket.

The Stuff Of Dreams Come True

IT began as a small item in the local paper. A large field directly opposite my living-room window had been bought by a builder and was to become a new housing estate.

I must admit the idea didn't appeal to me. For years I had enjoyed a view that had been the envy of all my friends.

In due course the surveyors came along, followed by diggers and bulldozers. Within a few months houses began to grow out of what had seemed like chaos. And all the time I was lamenting the loss of my lovely view.

Then something happened that changed everything — the people began to appear, to whom, one day soon, these houses were to become homes.

They came in the evenings after the workmen had finished for the day. In the main they were young couples. I could see them teetering along mucky gang planks to stand in what, in some cases, was simply a shell, and dream their dreams.

And as they dreamed of the future, I was thinking of the past. I was remembering my own first house . . .

I knew then exactly what they were thinking. They weren't seeing empty shells. They were seeing living-rooms filled with furniture, fitted kitchens and bathrooms.

Soon the first of the families will move in. Curtains will appear in the windows, and lights will gleam in the evenings.

I hear they are to have shops and a small playpark for the children — all the stuff of dreams come true.

And who am I to stand in the way of that?

"Well, I'm a bit pushed . . ." I lied. "I'm supposed to be meeting someone."

"Oh!" David said dully, and I knew I'd gone too far. "Perhaps another time then . . ." There was no life in his voice.

"All right, Dai," I said, not altogether letting him off the hook. He hated being called Dai. "I'll meet you outside at twelve o'clock. No later."

But the slight was lost on David. He nodded and gave me half a smile and backed out of the office.

The bell jingled again and I began typing the report. But I felt rebellious. If David thought I'd come running just whenever he pleased he was mistaken. I wasn't going to be used as a doormat, and I certainly wasn't going to be cornered into a polite, predictable sort of marriage just because other people willed it!

I thought of Colin, a bit wild, but free and able to cast his net further across the waters. We were going to motor over to Cenarth Falls that evening. I wanted to show him the genuine coracle fishermen.

I was proud of our local scenery although Colin didn't seem to notice it. He seemed to adapt to wherever he was at the time and nothing worried him. I had a sudden vision of his laughing, handsome face; he was so sure of himself, and yet a stranger.

I knew that he'd be returning to his Polytechnic in London in a few weeks, but he'd promised to write to me . . .

On the stroke of noon, I stepped out into the steep, cobbled street. David was waiting at the shop opposite.

He crossed the street with an apprehensive tread, as though he was out on his first blind date. We didn't seem like a couple who'd grown up together.

"Where shall we go?" David asked falteringly.

"I thought you would have decided that," I said sharply. But it was just as well he asked. I didn't want to risk bumping into Colin.

"Let's walk round by the quarry then," I suggested, firmly setting my feet in that direction.

"All right . . ." David said in disappointment. "I suppose it will be peaceful there, at least."

We walked down to the harbour road between the guest houses and the cafés, and there were discarded cockle cartons and ice lolly spatulas in the gutters.

"Not like it used to be in the old days, is it, Rhianon?" David said suddenly. And I knew he wasn't referring to the litter in the street.

SWN-Y-GWYLAN dropped abruptly out of sight and suddenly we were standing in the grim shadow of the slate quarry. It was an overpowering sort of place, haunting in its deathly stillness and greyness.

My father had sacrificed a lot of himself in this place, and I shivered.

Continued on page 138

I CAN'T think why you don't learn to drive a car," people often say to me. "Think how useful it would be."

They would never say this if, years ago, they had seen my efforts at cycling. If they had, they would be only too glad that I was not on the road driving such a lethal weapon as a car!

It all started when I was in school and my father rashly promised to buy me a bicycle if I learned to ride one first. He thought he was being smart there but he reckoned without Josie and Clanking Clara.

Josie was a school friend of mine, all legs and tightly curled hair, with a minute portion of gym slip in between.

Clanking Clara, her bicycle, was very tall and rusty and, as its name suggests — it clanked. But it was ideal for learning to ride on and Josie was a wonderful teacher, very patient and full of good advice.

When, finally, I learned to ride I went back to my father to ask him when I could expect to see the new bicycle.

ON A BICYCLE BUILT FOR ONE

Years ago cycling was one of my favourite pastimes, says Megan Boyes. And even now I have tender memories of those days in and out of the saddle!

He didn't believe me. So I borrowed Clanking Clara and away we went along the road before his amazed eyes.

We were well round the corner and out of sight when I fell off, so I got that new bicycle and she was duly christened Belinda.

MY most memorable ride on Belinda was to a friend's twenty-first birthday party, a distance of about four miles. Belinda and I went with a friend of mine called Jean, a proficient cyclist.

Somehow we managed to reach that party safely and got straight down to stuffing ourselves with unaccustomed chocolate éclairs and other goodies.

When the time came for Jean and me to go home, despite the gins we had drunk, we managed to scramble on to our cycles and off we went into the darkness, though not without the odd wobble.

It was now pitch black. As it was still wartime, there were no lights of any sort except the tiny beams that came through our hooded, blacked-out front lights. It looked as if it might be going to be an uneventful ride. I say looked, because just when we were congratulating ourselves on our good fortune, Hitler decided to launch a few V1s to make our journey more interesting!

The air was suddenly filled with a loud droning and the sky was cut by a red sinister trail. Then there was silence — followed by a ghastly "crump." Then the whole performance was repeated all over again.

Never have I cycled so quickly. I didn't even have time to spare for a wobble. One V1 tried to race us along the road until it finally gave up and fell with a thud somewhere to our right.

We reached Jean's home and I hastily waved aside her entreaties to come in and shelter for a while. Somehow I managed to ride the remaining half-mile between my home and Jean's.

THE war was over when I had my next big cycling experience. My fiancé and I were staying in the country with his sister.

Her husband was in hospital and she was rather anxious about some medical certificate or other which he had to have, so we said we would cycle to his doctor's to get it. I rode her bicycle and my fiancé rode her husband's.

It was then that I discovered the awful truth. What I had previously thought was Belinda's fault had been mine all along. This bicycle was playing even worse tricks than Belinda had done.

All might have been well if we hadn't had to go through the town, where it was Carnival Day. We didn't realise this until we saw the decorated streets lined with crowds of people and heard the strains of the town band.

On came the band and on I went. Then, before I quite knew what was happening, I was in the very middle of that band with trumpets and horns blowing in my ears from all sides.

At the very back came my fiancé, laughing his head off. I knew I couldn't expect any help from him, so I just had to go on until I could find a convenient turning. What the cheering crowd along the route thought I'll never know.

At last the turning came, and shame-faced I escaped down it, to be joined by my fiancé.

The band went serenely on and, to do them credit, they didn't miss one single note, though they were very likely as shaken by the whole affair as I was.

That experience unnerved me. That and the fact that more and more cars were coming on to the roads, making them unsafe for idiots like me.

Sadly, my cycling days were over. Belinda was laid to rest in my father's garage and the rust and cobwebs took over.

So I ask you, if I'm hopeless with a bicycle, what on earth would I be like in a car? The mind boggles. ■

Continued from page 135

"What did you want to see me about, David?" My voice sounded hollow.

His eyes restlessly scanned the rusted machinery on the quarry floor, abandoned, tyreless vehicles, chunks of awkward shaped slate, and the whitewashed slogans a quarter of the way up the face of the quarry wall, the handiwork of children and zealous nationalists.

David cleared his throat.

"We haven't been seeing each other lately, Rhianon."

Our voices were uncannily hollow in that dead place. If only he wasn't so embarrassed, so shy, I thought. If only he was more aggressive — and daring.

"I won't question your motives or feelings, Rhianon. I've given the matter a lot of thought and I've decided that I'm at fault. I've wronged you and wish to put things right as soon as possible."

My mouth must have dropped open for he glanced at me then looked away with a troubled frown, as though he'd overplayed his part.

"You? At fault, David?"

"Oh yes, Rhianon fach. I — I've been neglecting you. With my studies taking up so much time, I haven't been able to take you out much. And now this . . ."

He halted painfully, unable to mention Colin's name. I knew he suffered because of his shyness. If only he'd raised his voice at me, or stamped his foot or shook me hard, but he did none of these things. He angered me with being so polite and passive.

"I can go out with whoever I choose, David," I heard myself say stiffly. I was alarmed by the way I was feeling, guilty almost.

"I have decided, Rhianon . . ." David began.

I stared at him. He was studying the quarry face.

"I will not be going away to Lampeter, Rhianon," he continued, "I will stay in Swn-y-Gwylan and be a lobster fisherman like my father before me."

"But why, David?" My voice bit like a whiplash into the air.

"Because, Rhianon . . . because . . . I know we can't go on this way. A man can't keep his prospective bride feeling insecure for ever."

I gasped.

"Bride? Insecure? We've never had a moment's insecurity between us!" My face flushed in indignation.

"No, perhaps not," David said with hands clasped, looking for all the world like a preacher pontificating. "And I've never had the courage to mention marriage before."

I shrugged helplessly.

"Rhianon, I — I had to *believe* in us, can't you see?"

"Dai Hopkins, have you dragged me all the way up here just to . . . just to preach a sermon!"

"It was you who suggested coming here, Rhianon," he replied quietly. I felt my anger rise.

"Oh! David, stop it! Marry you? You've got the wrong person. I'm not made for a quiet wing of some dilapidated vicarage."

"But I'm not going to Lampeter, Rhianon," he said passionately. But by this time I was too angry to listen.

"Well, you ought to! You're not missing your vocation just for me. You're just trying to stop me going out with Colin Wilkes!"

There! I'd mentioned the unmentionable. And for the first time David's face reddened, and his speech held anger.

"Colin Wilkes! He's no good for you. He's only using you as his . . . his plaything until it's time to go back to London. No good can come of that, Rhianon."

BEWITCHED!

When my husband and I were on a bus tour of Scotland we went through some pine forests.

A French lady, on seeing some twig broomsticks for beating out fires, asked, "What are they for?"

"Witches like to have a nice fresh broomstick to fly on," my husband replied jokingly. "These are provided free by the Welfare State."

"Oh!" said the enchanted French lady, "you Scots think of everything!"

"You self-righteous . . . prig!" I yelled. "You sound just like my parents. Why don't you get down off your dignity for once . . . do something . . . drastic!"

Momentarily I stood aghast. I hadn't meant to go so far. I didn't even mean it.

David stood wide eyed, too shocked to reply.

"Well, if you'll excuse me!" I snorted. "You're taking up my lunch-hour."

I stormed off, away from the grey quarry, but David made no move, no sound. He let me go. And as I hurried back into the village, fuming and muttering, I realised that most of my anger was disappointment. David Hopkins had, in his own way, confronted me, and I'd rejected him. He had to let me go.

LATE afternoon I was hammering hard at my typewriter, head down, channelling all my annoyance into Mr Clegg's innocuous little letters, when the office bell jingled. I looked up with a scowl, then froze. Dad was standing there.

"Dad? What on earth are you . . ?" I began in a loud voice.

"You'd better come quick, Rhianon. It's David!"

"David?" I felt suddenly cold and stood up. "What about David?"

"He's had an accident. In the quarry."

My heart lurched. Mr Clegg came walking out of his office.

"What's happened, Dad?" I asked unsteadily.

My father turned to Mr Clegg.

"Rhianon will be leaving the office early today," he said firmly. "She's needed at home."

Mr Clegg stared, then nodded.

Instinctively I picked up my handbag, and I didn't even pause to put the cover on the typewriter.

I followed Dad outside and down the rickety stairs into the street.

"What's happened?" I said imploringly. "Is David all right?"

"He's broken his leg," Dad replied shortly. "As for your first question, Rhianon, I thought you'd be able to tell me."

"Me?"

"Yes. Why did David go to the quarry in the first place?"

We were walking along at a furious pace. It helped justify my reddening face somewhat.

"David's been taken to hospital," my father went on, without slackening his pace.

"Hospital? But that's twenty miles away, Dad!"

"I know. And I hope you'll be on your way there as soon as we've been to the quarry. There's something there you ought to see, Rhianon."

He didn't explain further. We went around the outcrop of overhanging rock and halted.

The quarry was deserted. But it was different. Something had changed.

I gazed upwards in wonder. Freshly whitewashed across the middle of the quarry face were huge, dripping white letters spelling out:

RHIANON MY LOVE

I gulped. Dad looked down at me and I blushed.

"Well, Rhianon? You tell me," he said mildly.

"Davi . . . David did that?" I croaked. He nodded.

"Uh-huh. Only how in this world he climbed right up there holding a pot of whitewash and a brush, I'll never know. It's a wonder he didn't break his back, not just a leg!"

Dad instinctively tensed his own back from his old quarry injury.

"David got a tin of whitewash and . . ?" I began and tailed off. I felt bewildered.

"He came into the chandler's shop asking if he could borrow some whitewash for a job he had to do," Dad explained. "He seemed upset — and determined, Rhianon. Said he was going to the quarry. I began worrying after he'd gone. So I strolled up there after a while and there he was, hanging on by his nails and daubing your name like some kind of madman."

"How did he fall, Dad?" I was breathless with shame.

"Once he'd finished daubing he must have lost his concentration." Dad shook his head, remembering. "Luckily there weren't any sharp rocks below."

I stared up at the rock face.

RHIANON MY LOVE

The lump in my throat seemed as big as a fishing float.

"I must go to David, Dad."

"I know. He kept saying your name when they were loading the stretcher into the ambulance. I couldn't get any sense out of him, though except —"

"Except?"

"Oh, nothing." He shrugged and turned me back the way we'd come. "Just something like . . . 'I hope that's drastic enough.' That makes sense to you, Rhianon?"

"Ye-es. That makes sense, Dad." We hurried back into the village.

"I'll just tell Mam where we're going," Dad said.

"I'll meet you by the harbour," I said. "I'll phone for a taxi while I'm waiting."

As I walked up and down waiting for Dad to come back I saw Colin Wilkes walking down the cliff road. He was chatting intently with another girl, a chambermaid at the hotel, I thought.

When he saw me, Colin stopped, looked sheepish, then hurried over to me.

"OK then, Rye?" he said, and he sounded embarrassed. "You still free for later?"

I looked coldly at him and wondered why I'd been such a fool.

"No, Colin, not today," I said firmly. Dad appeared then and we hurried up the street together.

"Wasn't that boy . . ." he began, but my frown silenced him.

"We'll get the taxi at the top of the hill, Dad," I said, "to save driving down through this maze of traffic. Trouble is with Swn-y-Gwylan there are far too many strangers here."

My father opened his mouth as if to speak, then grinned good-humouredly. He'd had me late in life but he understood a thing or two about a teenage daughter.

"I don't suppose David will be going to Lampeter now, Rhianon," he said, puffing as the gradient took its toll on us.

"No, Dad," I said with an enigmatic smile. "I don't suppose he will."

*** THE END ***

The Merry-Go-

"I'll remember this day as long as I live," she said. And, bemused and bewildered, her whole family nodded in silent agreement.

Complete Story by LAEL J. LITTKE

Round Of Love

MY sister Arlene was in love with the boy who operated the roundabout at the carnival which had recently come to Walker Park.

He had curly black hair and glowing-dark gipsy eyes. His name was Vincent. It didn't matter to Arlene that she knew absolutely nothing else about him.

The only thing was, Vincent didn't pay any attention to her. I suppose he was used to the worship of the girls who brought their little brothers, sisters, cousins or neighbours, so they — the girls — could sit on the nearby benches and watch him leap gracefully about the whirling horses.

Arlene thought he was divine. She said he looked like a film star and that the tinny waltzes that came from the centre of the roundabout provided a musical background for romance.

She took my brother, Billy, and me to the park so often that Billy became fed up with it and begged to be allowed to stay at home and play with his toy soldiers.

I thought he might as well. Vincent gave no indication that he ever even saw Arlene!

"I can't just walk right up and say, 'My name is Arlene, and I'd like to know you better,' " she said to me one day as we were cleaning up the room we shared.

"Why not?" I asked.

Arlene looked down at me with all the superiority a sixteen-year-old girl can feel over an eleven-year-old sister — and that's quite a lot.

"That just isn't the way you do it, Norma," she said slowly and patiently. Then she sighed. "When you grow up, you'll know why not."

"It would certainly save a lot of time," I said.

"You don't understand." Arlene flicked a duster across the top of her dressing-table, rearranging the dust. "If I could just get him to notice me!"

"You could leave a glass slipper there next time you go, and then he would come looking for you," I offered.

I was a Cinderella fan and considered anything less than princes and ball gowns and fairy godmothers unworthy of being called romance.

Arlene looked at me with something between pity and boredom.

"They don't make glass slippers any more," she said. Putting down the duster, she seated herself at the dressing-table and peered at herself in the mirror.

"Mirror, mirror, on the wall," I chanted in a high, squeaky voice, "who is fairest of them all?" Then I shifted to a deep voice to say, "Norma Pritchard is the fairest of them all."

Arlene turned round to throw a hairbrush at me. "You think you're so funny!" she said.

She turned back to the mirror. "I'm not really bad looking," she muttered, picking up a small bottle of perfume and sloshing some on her neck.

"That's it!" she exploded suddenly.

For a second I thought she had dropped the bottle.

"Why didn't I think of that before?" she said. She whirled around on the dressing-table stool. "I can't leave a glass slipper, but I could leave my little plastic purse with the set-in rhinestones. I could put this card with my name and address on it . . . and a lace handkerchief . . . and maybe fifty pence . . . so it would seem worth returning.

"He'd find it and bring it here to me, and, naturally, I'd have to invite him in for a cup of coffee or something, since he'd been so kind."

She leaned her elbows on her knees, day-dreaming.

"Well, let's go," I said.

"Go where?"

"To the park. Your purse isn't going to walk there alone." I looked at her with all the superiority a sensible eleven-year-old girl can feel over her boy-struck older sister — and that, too, is quite a lot.

Arlene jumped to her feet. "Get Billy," she instructed, dashing to her wardrobe to select a dress.

Billy, however, didn't want to go. "I'm sick of that roundabout," he said.

"You know Mum won't let us go to the park without you," I told him. I think she just liked to get us all out of her hair at once.

Billy sighed, putting away his toy soldiers.

Mum asked us to buy a chicken for dinner while we were out.

"Be sure to get it at Mr Simpson's," she said, "and be back here in plenty of time so I can cook it for dinner."

Mum always bought chickens from Mr Simpson's, where the plucked birds dangle by their legs in the front window. She says they taste far better than frozen birds.

We stopped for the chicken on the way to the park. Arlene said she didn't want to waste time on the way home, in case Vincent came right away to return her purse.

WHEN we got to the park, Billy wanted to play in the sandboxes near the swings. They were on the opposite side of the park from the roundabout, and Arlene had to bribe him with an iced lolly before he would come with us.

Vincent was wearing an orange shirt with a green-spotted neckerchief, and black jeans. Arlene thought the neckerchief made him look even more gipsyish and romantic than usual.

She put Billy and me on the roundabout for a ride, then found a bench where she could get a good view of Vincent and he could get a good view of her — if he happened to look that way.

She had changed her jeans and shirt for a scoop-neck white blouse and a bright skirt. She thought that Vincent's Romany blood would react more to the bright skirt.

As far as I could see, Vincent's Romany blood just lay there, calmly, in his veins. If he noticed Arlene at all, it certainly didn't show.

NO NEED TO TREMBLE...

One dark evening, a few weeks ago, my friend and I were sure we were being followed.

Rather scared, we stopped by a house where my friend stood inside the gate to pretend we were saying goodnight to each other. We thought this might frighten him away.

But the man who had followed us was not put off!

He came down the road and paused by the gate, where I was saying, "Well, goodnight..." in a loud voice.

"Excuse me," he said politely, and walked up the garden path to let himself in at his own door!

When the roundabout stopped, Arlene leaped aboard before we had a chance to get off.

"Stay on," she hissed, flourishing three tickets. "I'm going to ride, too."

The roundabout started, and our steeds began their monotonous gallop. The music thumped, and Vincent swung on to the moving platform.

Arlene licked her lips and adjusted her smile. She was perched sideways, and spread her full skirt out to cover her knees. After all, she didn't want to give him the wrong idea — not too much, anyway.

As Vincent approached, Arlene shoved the chicken at Billy. Somehow that lumpy parcel didn't fit in with the image she was trying to create.

Vincent didn't even pause as he took our tickets. He walked right on by, and the bright smile slid slowly from Arlene's face as he moved on to the next row of horses.

But she hadn't played her full hand yet!

"Billy!" she shrieked. "Don't do that! Billy, you'll fall off!"

Billy looked at her, puzzled. He was just sitting there, astride his horse, clutching the chicken.

Arlene reached over and grabbed his arm. "Billy!" she shrilled again.

Vincent turned around and came back.

"What's the matter?" he asked. He glanced briefly at Arlene, then concentrated on Billy.

"What's the matter, kid?" he repeated.

Arlene spoke up breathlessly. "I was afraid he was going to fall off."

"He was leaning 'way over," I put in, trying to be helpful.

Billy looked at us with all the icy disgust an eight-year-old brother can feel for two crazy sisters.

"I'm not a kid," he said to Vincent, with great dignity.

"Well, watch it, sonny," said Vincent, moving on.

MOROSELY, Arlene watched Vincent jump off the platform and settle himself in his canvas chair in the centre of the roundabout.

She was too occupied with her own thoughts to watch Billy, who was swinging the parcel containing the chicken round his head by the string.

As we passed Vincent, Billy took careful aim and let fly. The paper came off in midflight, and the limp, bare chicken landed squarely in Vincent's lap.

Arlene got off her horse and kept walking around, so that she stayed where Vincent couldn't see her during the rest of the ride. She made me go to retrieve the chicken when the roundabout stopped, hoping that Vincent wouldn't connect her with the incident.

Then she dropped her purse and hurried away.

I waited until Vincent was looking the other way, then I scooped up the chicken from the ground, and ran. I stopped only long enough to grab the paper, which I wrapped loosely around the bird before handing it to Billy to carry.

He carried it gingerly by the legs and lost the paper somewhere along the street.

"If he saw who threw that chicken, he won't ever come," Arlene said, her voice quivery, as if she was going to cry. But she said we would take the bus home, since she wanted to be sure to be there in case he did come.

The bus had been going for only three minutes when Billy said, "I feel sick."

The iced lolly, the roundabout, the swaying of the bus, and the sight of the chicken lying on his lap, had been too much for him.

He tossed the chicken on to the empty seat opposite, groaned weakly, and lay down. Arlene told me to open a window, while she started fanning him with her hands.

IN the excitement, we left the chicken on the bus.

"How could you possibly *lose* a chicken?" demanded Mum when we arrived home, pale and empty-handed.

"How can I worry about a chicken when my life is ruined?" asked Arlene.

"Well, dinner may be ruined, too!" said Mum.

Billy went a little paler and ran to his room to lie down.
"Who wants to eat?" said Arlene.
She was starting up the stairs, when the doorbell rang. Suddenly, she was Cinderella waiting for her prince. Her eyes, which had been filling with tears, sparkled with excitement.
"It's Vincent," she whispered. "He came!"
She sprinted to the door and flung it open. There stood a skinny twelve-year-old with buck teeth. In his outstretched hand, he held Arlene's little purse.
"Vincent said to take this to the scatterbrained female with the nasty brother and the dead chicken," he said.
Arlene just stood there.
"Thanks," I said, snatching the purse and slamming the door.
The doorbell rang again. The kid was still there, his hand still outstretched. "Cost me twenty pence on the bus," he said.
Arlene opened the purse and handed him twenty pence. I slammed the door again.
"Well, so much for Cinderella," I said.
"I want to die," whispered Arlene. She sank dramatically into a chair near the door.
Mother, who had been watching the whole scene, said, "Well, before you do, go and get another chicken." She went into the kitchen.
I was standing by Arlene's side, patting her back and hoping I'd never be sixteen, when the doorbell rang again. When I opened the door, I saw a tall blond boy with the bluest eyes I had ever seen. He held a package wrapped neatly in newspaper.
"Is your sister here?" he asked.
"Arlene," I called.
She got to her feet, tragedy still lining her face. She stared glassily at the boy.
"Hi," he said. "I brought your chicken." He handed the package to her."I was behind you on the bus, but I didn't see the chicken until you got off."
Arlene continued to stare at him, now with awakening interest.
"My name is Jeff," the boy said. "My family just moved in down the street." He grinned down at her rather shyly. "I've . . . I've been meaning to speak to you for the past few days . . ."
That was when Arlene came to completely. A dazzling smile erased the tragedy from her face.
"Why, Jeff," she said, "come on in and have a cup of coffee. Since we're neighbours now, we may as well get acquainted."
"I think so, too," Jeff said happily.
As they headed for the kitchen, I went upstairs to tell Billy he was a regular fairy godmother. After that, I planned to re-read my favourite version of Cinderella.

* **THE END** *

GOODBYE TO YESTERDAY

Brick by brick, over the years, she'd built a high, solid wall to shut out the past. Now a little boy's laughter brought it all tumbling down . . .

**Complete Story by
GRETA NELSON**

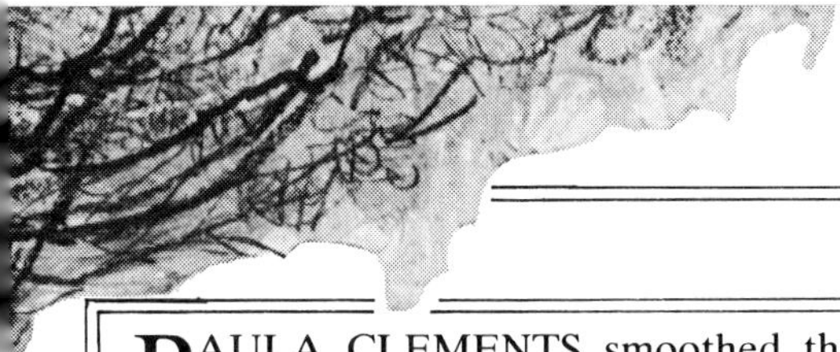

PAULA CLEMENTS smoothed the velvet folds of the drawing-room curtains for what must have been the tenth time that morning. She looked out through the latticed windows at her garden, taking in the immaculate lawn, and her precious roses, still wet with dew. Her beautiful, peaceful garden that gave her strength, and comfort.

Her eyes flickered over the high wall covered with creeper. She'd had four years to practise ignoring that wall; four years to push its dreadful memories further and further back in her mind. And she'd won. Now it was just a wall, draped in bright red creeper.

Paula looked at the bright border of lupins and dahlias, admired the brave beds of begonias, then she found her gaze straying to the wall again. How odd, she thought impatiently, that today of all days it should be so difficult to maintain her usual detachment. Today, when she should be knee-deep in planning details for a visit of three total strangers.

At morning service one Sunday the Reverend Mr Dinning had asked her if she could take part in this holiday scheme for needy people. She was practically the only person in the village who hadn't volunteered her services over the years. Face to face with him, she'd said a very reluctant yes — and had been regretting it ever since.

She shuddered again at the thought. Three strangers sharing her life, her home, her solitude for five days. How unbearable. Perhaps not completely unbearable if only they didn't probe . . .

The creeper on the wall was quite thick now after four years of steady growth. It was glossy and strong with a tentacle-hold. The pretty maroon-coloured leaves hid the monstrosity of bricks. She had demanded that wall immediately after the awful accident.

Her husband, Ian, as grief-stricken as she was, had complied with her every wish, had indulged and pampered her. She had devoured all the comfort he had to give and knew she had offered nothing in return.

Paula looked down and saw the bruises on the cerise curtains, flattened dents of velvet where her fingers had clutched. She glanced at the clock. It was nearly half-past eleven. They'd be here any minute. There was just time to check on lunch. She'd decided on chicken fricassee and mousse to follow.

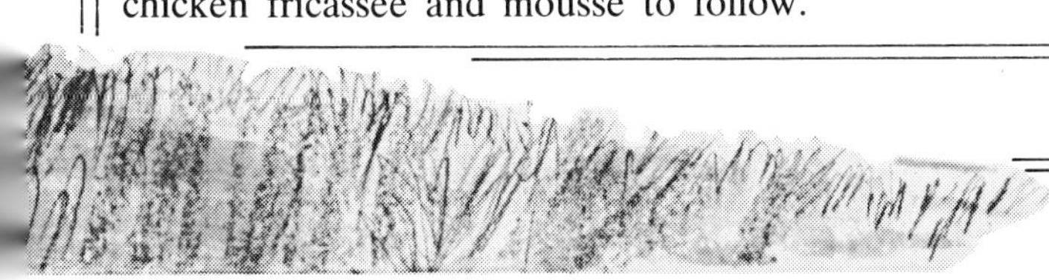

The kitchen, like the rest of the house was spacious, uncluttered and luxurious. The fricassee looked perfect and the vegetables waited, crisp and appetising.

PAULA felt the first flicker of interest. It might be fun to cook for guests again.

Ian had stopped bringing people home. He booked a table in town if he had clients to entertain and she didn't question it. She couldn't remember the last time she'd really talked to Ian. Oh, they discussed things politely enough — the weather, world affairs, which holiday they would choose. But they avoided anything personal.

That's the way it had been ever since that agonising day, four years ago; the day, Gordon, their eighteen-month-old son, drowned in the fish pond.

In the days following the funeral, Paula nearly went mad with grief, hurling abuse at everyone around her, but most of all blaming herself for what had happened.

Ian had sympathised with her and loved her. But she could not respond.

She refused to move house but she did demand the wall; six foot of red brick with a filled-in, cemented-over ornamental pool at the other side.

Paula put the vegetables on to simmer. She was trembling and the water spilt, hissing dementedly into little spitting blobs all over the cooker. She wiped it up automatically and felt a sudden anger at her slipping of control.

She'd not allowed herself to think like this for years. It must be these wretched people coming.

She tried to concentrate on the day before her.

She felt the trembling subside as she checked the place mats and napkins on the dining-room table. Her red candles added colour and interest and the polished rosewood sparkled.

Then she heard the car at the gate. Punctual at least, she thought, pleased that one irritation had been avoided.

She felt almost eager as she went through the hall to greet them. She opened the front door and stared in open-mouthed disbelief at the clutter of cases, paper carriers and their owners — three children of varying ages.

The Reverend Arthur Dinning beamed at Paula and went on beaming even in the face of her icy silence.

"Surprise, surprise," he said cheerfully. "We have a new age allocation this time. And you have three very excited guests."

Paula felt the panic rise in her throat as she looked at the children, two boys and a girl.

She said carefully, "Mr Dinning, I would prefer the normal age allocation. I have catered and planned exclusively for old people. My husband —"

Arthur Dinning ushered his little brood on to the grass and returned to Paula.

"I'm sure your husband would agree, Mrs Clements. The children have slept, talked and dreamed of nothing else but this holiday for months. You can't ruin it for them, can you? Besides, their mother went into hospital last week."

Paula realised he was watching her closely. She looked at the children. They were silent, waiting. How could she bear a week of it? A week of shouting and tumbling and play, a week of what might have been.

"I feel the whole thing is most unfortunate. You should have let me know!" But she was already picking up the bags. She had a feeling he had known exactly what her reaction would be.

Arthur Dinning stayed long enough to see the children settled at lunch and then he left. She was alone. She would have to cope with her unwelcome guests on her own.

★ ★ ★ ★

As Paula closed the front door behind the vicar, and returned to the dining-room, she felt like a stranger in her own house. The sound of quarrelling voices ceased immediately she entered the room.

The two elder children, a girl and a boy, had already finished their first course. The little boy sat, his fluffy fricassee congealing, intact.

Paula ignored this and said, "We'd better introduce ourselves properly. I'm Mrs Clements and you'll meet my husband this evening."

The girl was spokeswoman. "I'm Sylvia Howard. I'm twelve. They're my brothers, Lawrence and Georgie."

"Are you ready for your pudding?" Paula asked.

"What is it?" demanded Sylvia and Lawrence at once.

"It's mousse," Paula said. "Like ice-cream."

"Moose!" spluttered Lawrence. "I ain't eatin' antlers." His wit produced a spell of uncontrollable coughing and laughter.

Georgie, by now, definitely looked a bit grey and his bottom lip trembled ominously.

That's all I need, Paula thought, a home-sick child.

Georgie revealed in the next moment that it was a physical and not an emotional sickness. And after she'd cleaned him up, put him in the small bedroom to rest, mopped up and disinfected the injured piece of Indian carpet, she made herself a cup of coffee.

The other two children, still slightly subdued, were walking slowly, aimlessly, round the garden, occasionally stopping to examine the flowers.

Paula sipped her coffee and on impulse rang Ian's office. She could hear the surprise in his voice. Small wonder. She hadn't rung him for years. She could hear the tension in her own voice as she gave him the news.

"Look, if you feel you *can't* manage, they'll have to go," Ian was saying carefully, but she didn't think he'd have been too pleased if she agreed.

"They're installed now. One's already been sick all over the dining-room carpet. And heaven knows how many breakages there'll be." Her voice was steady now.

"Look. I'll try to be home early. Are you sure you can cope?"

"Yes, of course," she said, and heard the conviction in her voice.

SHE rang off and went upstairs to see how Georgie was faring. He was asleep, lying across the bed with his feet dangling over the edge. She moved him slightly and pulled the cover over him. Nice little face, she thought, smoothing back his hair. Not too clean, but such a nice little face.

She went downstairs and sorted through all the games and entertainments she'd hunted out for her elderly guests. Chess — that was no good. Solitaire — too dull probably.

Putting Together The Past

I WAS half-way through the long-overdue task of clearing out a hall cupboard the other day when I came on an old attaché-case.

Curious, I blew off the dust and snapped open the catches.

Among other odds and ends inside was a battered cardboard box. There was no picture on the front, but inside were the pieces of a jigsaw puzzle.

It was then I rediscovered an old obsession of my youth — doing jigsaws. For immediately the task of clearing the cupboard was forgotten.

Picking my way carefully along the junk-strewn hall, I sat down at the living-room table.

It wasn't easy without a picture to follow, so I began as I'd always done, by completing the outside edge.

Then slowly, painstakingly, I filled in a corner here and part there until slowly a scene began to appear — and with it a thousand long-forgotten memories.

The scene was of a part of Wales my parents had taken me on the first holiday I can remember.

My father had bought the puzzle for me, and together over the years we'd sat on rainy Sunday afternoons happily piecing together the puzzle and reliving our holiday.

And now, so many years later (I'm not saying how many), there I sat, reliving it all again.

The cupboard was cleared in the end and the rubbish thrown out.

The jigsaw? It's back safe and sound — in the cupboard.

Heavens, if it was wet, she would need paints and cut-outs. She'd take the children into the village later and get some things.

She watched Sylvia and Lawrence sitting outside on the lawn. They looked so dejected and lost that Paula was prompted to action. She opened the window.

"Why don't you pull me some raspberries? They're over there by the peonies. Come and get a bowl, Sylvia. We'll have raspberries and cream for tea."

The children instantly sprang to life, running towards her and, Paula thought guiltily, they're hating it more than I am. They expected a house of fun and games and I've disappointed them.

Georgie had recovered, so she drove them all into the village before tea. They piled out of the car and waited politely for her.

Paula consulted her list. "We want paints, lots of cardboard, playing cards, and maybe some comics," she told them.

Miss Beech, the postmistress, watched with interest as Paula and the three children approached.

"Do you stock paints and colouring books, Miss Beech?" Paula asked, and she felt she might as well be asking for live alligators. Miss Beech responded admirably and showed not a whit of surprise as she brought out a selection.

"Your holiday guests, Mrs Clements?" she asked.

"Yes, they arrived today. Our air should do them so much good," Paula said, and realised that it was the longest conversation she'd ever had with Miss Beech.

The children were making life or death decisions among the materials laid out on the counter and Georgie, who appeared to be quite aggressive when completely well, elbowed Sylvia in the ribs. She promptly hit him with the paint-box she was examining. Paula hastily intervened and eventually got them out to the car, fully conscious that passers-by were looking at them in astonishment.

PAULA was in the garden when Ian arrived home that evening but she knew exactly what he'd find indoors. The appalling noise would lead him upstairs to the bathroom.

When she'd left the children, Sylvia was brandishing loofah and soap and two soapy heads were peering over the bath. The perfect order of the pink-tiled bathroom was well and truly sabotaged.

Ian was coming downstairs when Paula went in, carrying an assortment of wellington boots.

"The ground's a bit damp in the woods. These were in a mess."

Ian nodded. "So's the bathroom, Paula, it's not too late to say no."

She busied herself at the cooker. "Oh, it is too late, Ian. Their mother's in hospital. We'll just have to accept it. It's only for a week."

Paula quickly laid place mats on the Formica-topped kitchen bar. "We'll eat in here, if you don't mind. They're a bit over-awed in the dining-room. Too much polished furniture."

Ian grunted. "I noticed the patch on the carpet. How is he?"

Paula sorted cutlery. "Georgie? He's fine. It was just car sickness. And he didn't eat any lunch, so I expect he'll be starving."

Ian said, "Me too! What is it?"

Paula took the plates from the hot drawer. "Fish fingers and chips." Her eyes met Ian's defiantly. "Georgie," she added, "loves chips."

This last statement was admirably illustrated as Georgie, with inelegant but enthusiastic relish, cleared his plate. He was shining and mint-new from his bath, and his fair hair had dried attractively into bouncing curls. What a nice little face, Paula thought again.

After the meal, the children took Ian into the dining-room to show him the things she'd bought them that afternoon. Paula, from the kitchen, heard the occasional bursts of laughter and she felt a sudden envy that Ian should apparently find it so effortless.

They were playing ludo when she went in, spiritedly and noisily. Georgie, a consistent loser, knocked the board over in a moment of frustrated pique, and received a slap from Sylvia. Ian cut in and hoisted the tearful Georgie on to his shoulders.

"Bed is the order of the day. No arguments. Bed for all of you. First days are extremely tiring, and we want you fresh and bright-eyed for tomorrow."

The children responded immediately, and, headed by Ian, they trooped upstairs.

SIGN OF THE TIMES

What has happened to the marvellous autograph albums which friends once inscribed so lovingly? Many people used to draw exquisite pictures and print beautiful poems in them.

Have we no time for sentiment today?

It almost seems we don't want to recall the dozens of friends we once had!

Paula sat in the lounge and closed her eyes. How tired she was! But not an unpleasant tiredness, she realised, and wondered if she could dispense with her sleeping pill tonight. She regarded Ian through half-closed lids as he came in.

"Nice bunch of kids," he said. "Tough little beggars, but I reckon their parents can congratulate themselves. What's wrong with their mother?"

Paula shrugged. "Mr Dinning didn't say. Sylvia says it's a 'woman's complaint,' so take your pick." She watched him for a moment or two. "They like you."

Ian smiled. "Because I let them cheat at ludo."

Paula shook her head. "No, they like you. They don't feel easy with me."

Ian Clements lit a small cigar, then he said, "It's always easier for the men of the house. We come home when all the work's done, when the chips are ready! We come when the fun commences."

Their eyes met and for a second Paula knew he'd meant to make her feel better but instead she was overcome with shame and guilt. The evenings of these past few years couldn't have been much fun for him, she thought.

All she said was, "Heavens knows what we'll do tomorrow."

"I'll take the day off if you like," Ian said. "We'll all go to the zoo or if it's a nice day, maybe the beach. We'll take a vote at breakfast tomorrow."

ZOOS apparently were two a penny in the Hindlesbury vicinity but beaches were a scarcity and the children's vote was unanimous.

As luck had it, it was one of the nicest days they'd had for ages and the children helped Paula to pack the car with deckchairs and the windbreaker.

She was filling the two picnic hampers when Sylvia dashed through the kitchen on some errand. "Pity you haven't got a bucket," she said. "Bucket and spade. Georgie wants to make sandpies."

Paula fastened the catch on the second hamper carefully.

"We can always buy one when we get there," she said. Her voice was calm but she felt the despair rise in her, and suddenly the warmth of the sun and the high expectation of the day before her evaporated.

For she was remembering another seaside expedition. A carefree day full of laugher with baby Gordon. They'd bought him a bucket and spade but he'd been too young, and it had been upstairs in the attic ever since, still shiny and new.

She forced herself to check the food again, running through a list of essentials, and by the time they set off, she was easier again.

She was silent during the drive but Ian and the children made up for her with their sing-song. He taught them "On The First Day Of Christmas" and "Green Grow The Rushes O" and they sang skipping rhymes and football supporters' chants.

Ian chose a long narrow stretch of beach. It was quite deserted and the children whooped through the dunes.

Ian lifted the chairs and windbreaker on to the grass.

"Can you manage the rest, Paula?" he asked her. He was making for the cove already weighed down.

Paula turned to the boot and froze. All that was left were the picnic baskets — and a bucket and spade, spanking new and colourful, slightly filmed with four years of attic dust.

She picked up the food hampers and caught up with Ian.

"That's Gordon's bucket and spade," she said accusingly. "How *could* you?"

He strode on. "It'll be put to better use here than it has been lying idle in the loft for four years."

Ian's eyes met Paula's defiantly and he offered her no words of comfort as he got down to securing the windbreaker.

Continued on page 158

In The Shadow Of ETNA

For the Pecorellis, Sicily promised to be all sunshine and laughter. Then Mount Etna stirred and began to breathe fire . . .

CARNIVAL time in Sicily — that is what we were promised by our Italian friends, Margherita and Renato, when we stayed with them in Taormina. And though we looked forward to this very much we didn't realise that this was to be the holiday of a lifetime in a way we could scarcely have guessed.

The first day passed with great gaiety as my husband Giuseppe and I with three of our four children, Marie-Louise, Daniel and Nicholas, watched the carnival procession go by.

The narrow steep streets of Taormina rose from the glittering blue sea and everywhere was a riot of flowers in bloom.

Gaily plumed and sequinned horses were dancing in time to the cheery flutes, tambourines and drums played by Sicilians dressed in bright, colourful local costumes.

The day was full of lightness — gaiety and sunshine — but the evening turned out to be utterly different. For Etna, which usually lies so calm and silent above the Sicilian countryside, had yet again burst into life.

Although our children were all under seven, we felt that they should not miss a unique occasion. So we set off up the smoke-shadowed slopes of the great volcano.

The main road was blocked by the lava and so we had to go up a bumpy mountain track normally used only by lorries.

The fiery mountain had looked very near to us in Taormina, but it took an hour to climb up in the car, past yellow broom and chestnut trees in the gathering twilight.

Quite a crowd had the same idea as ourselves and the road was packed with cars and people on foot, all aiming for the deepening red glow in the distance.

Our excitement grew as night fell and the glow from the fire on the horizon drew us forward as if it were some great magnet.

We left the road and drove over tracks of mud and sometimes lava that had come down the mountain only days previously.

Already, it was hardening into grey, lumpy crust. Movement was slow and painful as streams of cars passed one another on tracks made only for donkeys.

When we could drive no further we got out of the car and climbed gingerly in the dark up the dusty hill. We kept tight hold of the children, at the same time desperately clinging to bushes to stop ourselves from slipping. It was pretty tough going.

As we approached the moving stream of lava the heat grew intense and acrid smoke billowed in the air around us. Dust and the fumes made our eyes sting.

By PENNY PECORELLI

Then, in a moment, we were there, barely five feet away from the burning stream.

IMAGINE, for a moment, in a kind of nightmare, the fire in your living-room magnified a thousand times, advancing slowly, relentlessly towards you. The heat drives in solid waves, your eyes seared by the brightness.

This river of fire, perhaps twenty yards wide, shimmered in the darkness, the masses of red hot lava falling in cascades like a waterfall.

As we stood watching, the children silent with wonder, I imagined with a shiver of horror how the inhabitants of ancient Pompeii must have felt as just such a torrent of fire swept towards them.

In the darkness we stumbled back to where our car was parked and rather thankfully headed down to low ground and normal life.

The following day, Margherita took us to the point the lava had reached in its relentless slide down the mountain.

Several places had had miraculous escapes, the lava turning away from them when only a few feet away, and destruction seemed absolutely inevitable.

We saw, for instance, a hotel perched on a crag and completely isolated by the flow of lava.

And still, as we watched, the huge mass rolled down between two high hills. By that time, Renato said, it had covered many houses, vineyards, orange and lemon groves.

For the people of the region it was, of course, a major catastrophe.

We stopped to talk to an old man. As we chatted he went on watering his small vineyard almost as if nothing special was happening.

I asked him how he could stay on when the threat of losing everything hung over him.

He stood there in the sun and looked towards the area quite near to his precious vineyard where the lava flow was making the vegetation smoke and flame. He wiped his brow and narrowed his eyes.

"It is our life," he told me. "What else can we do but hope it will not be us?

Continued from page 155

Paula, her eyes closed against the sun, sat apart from them all. She heard the laughter and squeals of delight and felt shut out.

She felt a light touch on her arm. Georgie, his sturdy little body covered with sand. "I's hungry," he said.

Paula looked at him. His round cheeks were already browned by the sun and his eyes were searching hers. His hand was still on her arm, the small fingers opening and closing on her wrist.

"Peter Abbott's mum went into hospital and she never came back. They put her in the ground."

Paula felt shock at his matter-of-fact tone which concealed the fear in his eyes all too clearly.

"*My* mum'll come home, won't she?"

"Of course she will, Georgie," Paula assured him and she put her arm round him and hugged him tight.

"My mum would like this beach." The thought cheered Georgie up. "She makes smashing sandpies." The entreaty was blatant.

"Bring the bucket and spade, Georgie," Paula said quietly.

The newness of the shiny red and blue pail was already a thing of the past, and Paula took it unflinchingly. "Right!" she said. "We want dampish sand, and we need to pack it tightly. We'll make some sandpies even your mum would approve of."

When Ian broke off the game of beach cricket and suggested food, Paula and an oddly-attired Georgie were sitting happily in a circle of perfectly-formed sandpies.

He smiled at her. "I knew you could do it," was all he said.

The rest of the day went with a swing and when they arrived home Paula rang the vicar and he assured her that Mrs Howard's operation had been successful and that she would be home in ten days' time.

"How are you coping?" he asked curiously. He seemed pleased by her reply.

"I knew you could do it, Mrs Clements," was all he said before he rang off.

It was only when she had put the phone down that Paula realised they had both used exactly the same words.

The children of course were delighted by the news and after hot baths all round they went contentedly to bed.

Continued from previous page

"If it is," he added with a resigned look, "we start again."

Wherever the flows of lava wound downwards towards the sea, people stood staring at the hypnotic sight. Yet, strangely, while this drama of life and death was going on up the mountain, the dancing and gaiety still went on far below in the streets of the coastal town.

But then that is the Italian character — bubbling with the joy of living, enjoying the drama of even the most threatening situations.

Certainly none of us will ever forget the sunshine — and the shadows — of that unforgettable holiday. ■

AT breakfast next morning Paula suggested that the children should write to their mother, and after much discussion Sylvia wrote the letter, Lawrence drew a picture and Georgie enclosed his favourite shell from the outing to the beach.

Paula included a short note, giving her best wishes and saying how well the children were. Then Ian was duly entrusted with the precious envelope and Paula walked with him to the car.

"Will you be all right?" he asked. "It's going to be a long day."

"Yes, I'll be fine." She looked away from his gaze. There was so much to say to make up for the last four numbed years but now, she knew, was not the time to say it. She smiled. "We'll be fine," she repeated. "Don't worry."

The week flew by. The children relaxed and became expansive, confiding and trusting. Sylvia attempted great changes in Paula's appearance.

"You're so pretty!" she said despairingly. "But you never bother with your hair and things like that. Mum has hers done every week, and she has it bleached. She's really quite dark, you see. Dad gets hopping mad 'cause it's so expensive, but Mum likes it. And she wears her things nice and short."

Paula was amused and allowed herself to be bullied into shortening hemlines, and even into crocheting a waistcoat. One day, on impulse, she bought heated rollers. Sylvia was excited and insisted that she should try them out as soon as they got home.

When Ian arrived, Sylvia greeted him at the door. "Fashion show!" she said excitedly, pulling him into the lounge and pushing him into an armchair.

"And here we have Paula wearing a hostess gown with her hair styled by Sylvia," she said dramatically as Paula stood in the doorway.

"I feel a bit silly," Paula said self-consciously.

Ian stood up. "What an odd choice of words. You look beautiful."

He went over to her. Her face was flushed with embarrassment. Her hair was soft and shining with feathery tendrils brushing on to her cheeks. "In fact, you look stunning," he said.

In that moment Paula remembered the good times they'd had together; she remembered how close they used to be.

She looked away. "I'll get the meal," she said, "and meanwhile Sylvia can chat *you* up into becoming more trendy!"

ALL too soon the day for the children's departure arrived and over breakfast there was a false gaiety, too much talk and too much bickering between them.

Ian promised to come back for lunch to see them off, and after he'd left, the children hung around the kitchen looking lost.

"Why don't you go out into the garden?" Paula suggested. "I know, pick some flowers to take home. I don't mind what you choose. Honestly!"

She gave them scissors and her flower basket and smiled to herself as Sylvia, as usual, took charge. Then she went upstairs to see to their packing. Sylvia had already completed hers, but the boys' room was in a mess.

She was going to miss them so much, their noise, their uncomplicated chatter, the sense of release they had provided between Ian and herself.

They were quiet enough at the moment, she mused. It was then she heard the cry. Two cries to be exact; one of fear and the other, an urgent cry for help. It was Sylvia's voice shouting for her.

She met the girl halfway down the staircase. Sylvia's face was white and she was near tears. "It's Georgie!" she shouted. "He's fallen off the wall! He's on the other side."

Paula's heart missed a beat, then she was running. She stopped at the garage for the extending ladder and half-dragged, half-carried it to the other end of the garden.

Lawrence, pale and uncomfortable, said, "He wanted me to leg him up, and then he saw some flowers on the other side. He wanted to give them to you and he fell."

The anxiety and guilt in the round, freckled face was plain to see. "Don't worry, Lawrence," she said. "Just hold the ladder steady. Right?"

Georgie was lying on the concrete, one leg doubled up ominously. He wasn't unconscious, and when he saw Paula, great tears ran freely down his face. She knelt beside him.

"Oh, Georgie, Georgie! I think you've broken your leg. We'd better get a doctor," she said.

He clutched at her and she said gently, "I'll get Sylvia to phone. I promise I shan't leave you. Not for a moment."

She shouted instructions to Sylvia to ring for the doctor and Ian, and she sat beside Georgie, stroking his hands and smoothing his hair.

"I saw the flowers and you hadn't any like them in your garden. I wanted to give you something different." He pointed to the giant king-cups, yellow and glossy-bright in the morning sun.

The king-cups from the pool, she thought in amazement. They'd forced their way through the concrete, seeking for themselves light and sun and life. And they had succeeded — just as she had succeeded, with a little help from Ian and Mr Dinning . . .

Georgie felt the hot, wet drops on his face. "You're crying," he said. "You're cross about the flowers."

Paula held him to her. "I'm not cross, Georgie. Not in the least cross."

But she didn't attempt to check her tears, for she knew they were the beginnings of her survival, her return to warmth and love.

* **THE END** *

MY TWO WINGED "WATCHDOGS"

BY MARION A. STOCKS

IT was spring and we were living in a caravan about three yards from the edge of a large lake. The lake was a favourite site for all the keen anglers from miles around.

As well as the fish, the lake was also the home of two beautiful swans, which we soon nicknamed Charlie and Floss.

Our caravan was quite some way away from all the others on the site and our four-year-old daughter, Lenna, had to be constantly watched in case she got too near the water, or wandered off across the fields.

Charlie, the male swan, was very

cautious of approaching us at first, and viewed us all at a distance. I began coaxing him with pieces of bread, which I threw into the water for him.

Floss, who had a much more placid nature than her mate, took no coaxing at all, and floated around gracefully two or three feet away from me, accepting all that was offered, much to Charlie's annoyance.

Having broken through their reserve, I fed them three or four times a day. They soon began to expect those daily handouts.

It wasn't long before Charlie thought he might do a little better for himself, so out of the water he lumbered. I was a bit taken aback at this, as I had heard that swans can be funny at times. My daughter happened to be some distance away, so I fed Charlie by hand, and at the same time called to her.

By the time Lenna had got back into the caravan, Floss had also got out of the water, but she didn't wait for the bread to be proffered, she just took it from my fingers.

My daughter was delighted and promptly wanted to try it for herself. Needless to say, I didn't want her to, as the swans stood as high as her. But no sooner was my back turned than she was outside trying it for herself.

I watched her; and it was comical to see her offer the bread only to bring her hand back smartly as soon as a beak came forward to take it. Funnily enough, the swans seemed to realise that she was a little frightened of them, and took the bread very carefully from the palm of her hand.

One morning, whilst hanging out some washing, I heard a dog yap-yapping at something or someone. That someone was Lenna. The dog was running round and round her, and yapping like mad at the same time.

Charlie and Floss were over our side of the lake at the time and Charlie was out of the water like a flash.

He stood up on his feet, spread his wings, and went straight for the little dog, flapping his wings furiously as he went forward. I was terrified. One good smack from those huge flapping wings and Lenna could be badly hurt.

But Charlie seemed to know what he was doing. As I watched, he lured the little dog away from Lenna. It was like watching a fencing match.

The thrust and parry of Charlie's neck was sharp and decisive, and so was his beak, too, as I gathered from the cries that came from the dog. The animal soon realised that he wasn't welcome, called it a day, and went off.

Charlie's ruffled feathers soon smoothed themselves down again, but he didn't go back into the water again for some time. He looked as if he was standing guard, waiting for the little dog to come back again.

AFTER that Charlie and Floss really became our friends. One morning we were woken up by a continuous tap-tapping on the side of the caravan, underneath the window where we slept.

My husband, thinking he had overslept, jumped out of bed, and I looked out of the window. I was quite amused, and called to my husband to come and see the cause of the tapping.

"Well, I'll be blowed," he said. "No need to set the alarm clock if they are going to knock us up in the morning." And that is just what they did do, every morning as regular as clockwork. Nothing would move them until I had fed them.

As there were no shops nearby, I had to go to the nearest village. Always on returning, the two swans would be sitting on the bank, near the end of the caravan. I was uneasy at first in case they wouldn't let me pass, but as I walked closer they would get up and waddle back into the water.

Unfortunately the same technique didn't work for strangers. The milkman, the postman and the paperman all came in for Charlie's clear-off treatment.

Whatever Happened To Simple Peace and Quiet?

I OFTEN ask myself that question. Indeed I ponder on it at least a dozen times a day . . . usually when I feel numb from an overdose of noise. I could be wrong, but I swear that the level of noise in everyday life seems to grow higher with every passing day.

Take traffic, for example. A great deal of money and effort on the part of car manufacturers has resulted in cars with more silent engines. In theory, that is.

In practice, five minutes at the edge of a pavement in the middle of any busy town will leave you deafened and irritated by the roar of traffic!

Workplaces are much the same. Factories seem to have twice the machinery (and four times the noise) of years gone by . . . the large stores which have replaced so many small shops seem crowded with shoppers, each of whom contributes hum and hubbub to the noise level . . . and offices are filled with the latest in typewriters, duplicators, computers — all of which click and clatter in deafening unison.

Steal away from it all for a quiet cup of tea somewhere . . . and what does one find? "Canned music" playing "softly" in the background! And everyone talking that little bit louder in order to make themselves heard!

If only there was a simple solution to it all. A means to cut out all noise. Ah, the peace and quiet would be deafening!

As soon as any of these people showed up, Charlie would be out of the water as quick as a flash, stand right up on his feet, spread his wings out and slowly move forward.

Those people would naturally avoid coming into contact with those wings of Charlie's, so that meant I had to go up to the paddock, a hundred yards or so away, to collect my milk and anything else that had been left for me!

About that time we began to notice that Charlie was often on his own, although Floss would come across occasionally. Being curious about this, I took a walk round to the far side of the lake, where I had often seen them landing.

I came to the spot, and stopped and looked around. In front of me was another very small lake, and in the middle, there was Floss, sitting on a huge nest.

Charlie was there, too. Although he didn't attempt to move me off, he didn't encourage me either. He stood between me and the nest, swaying from side to side like a pendulum in a clock.

After my visit to the nest, we didn't see so much of our guardians during the day, although they still came across first thing in the morning.

It was shortly after my visit to the nest that I saw in our local paper a huge photograph — of Charlie and Floss, with their family, nine of them, out on the lake.

Later we sold the caravan, and as we were giving it a good going over, prior to selling it, we found the marks and scratches underneath the window where they had come so regularly for their breakfast.

Charlie and Floss had certainly left their marks, in more ways than one. ■

Complete Story by
RHODA ELIZABETH PLAYFAIR

That

Funny, isn't it, how all the Christmas cards and gifts in the world aren't nearly as precious as simply knowing that someone really cares for you?

IT'S funny, but at Christmas, people seem to do the oddest things. Like the thing Stewart Gregory Waterford did one Christmas when he was working as a relief postman.

"Of all the stupid things to do," was the way Greg put it.

Everyone called him Greg except Martha. Martha called him Gregory, sounding all three syllables. The way Martha pronounced *any* three syllables was enough to make him feel ten feet tall.

It was because of Martha that he took the Christmas relief job at the post office, delivering parcels. Second-year Engineering students on a grant don't have money for extra-special Christmas gifts, and he wanted Martha's to be really extra special.

He thought about it while he went round with his parcels, twice a day. Some of the hand-made pottery she liked. Or one of those beautifully-bound art books she admired — Martha was an art student. Anything really, as long as it was special . . .

It was snowing when he made his first delivery to Mrs Webster's nursing home. There was snow in feathery piles along the hand-rail of the bridge as he crossed it to get to River Avenue.

Special Feeling

He could tell at once that it was a friendly place. The cleaning lady in the front hall, nodded in friendly fashion and said, "Will you wait a minute, please? I'll call Ellen!"

When Ellen, a plump motherly soul, arrived and saw the parcels for Mrs Clarke and Mrs Donaldson, her face lit up.

"My, aren't they lovely?"

She took them from Greg, and carried them across the room.

"They go straight under the tree! Everything —" she paused to beam at Greg "— straight under the tree — until Christmas Eve."

He hadn't bothered to look at the tree before, but he did now. It stood in a tiny alcove beside the stairs. It was because he was half-turned towards it that he didn't notice the old woman approaching him until she was very close and peering up at him through owl-like lenses.

"Ronnie?" Her old voice question-marked the name. "Iss that you, Ronnie? So! *Wie geht's?*"

"It isn't Ronnie, Mrs Schwartz."

The old face saddened in its lines as Ellen took her arm. "Not Ronnie?"

"No. She thinks you are her nephew," Ellen said. "She's almost blind."

She raised her voice. "He brought some parcels, Mrs Schwartz. See? You can see the ribbon."

She lifted the box marked, *Mrs Clarke. Don't open until Christmas!* and placed it in the old hands.

"Iss beautiful!" said Mrs Schwartz, and Greg went whistling on his way.

It was late the following day before he had to call back at the nursing home. The snow had stopped and darkness had already enveloped the fat evergreens stretching between Mrs Webster's and the river.

He climbed the steps with parcels for Mrs Brown, Mrs Trent, and a second one for Mrs Donaldson.

Ellen said, "My! Every one looks different! Aren't we lucky?"

And Mrs Schwartz shuffled towards him in her soft red slippers and said, "Ronnie? Iss that you? *Wie geht's?*"

"That Ronnie!" Ellen said, her brown eyes angry. "He never comes to see her and she has no-one else. I suppose you must be about his size."

"That's OK," said Gregory, and went about his business.

HE mentioned it to Martha, however. They were both busy during the week, but he telephoned every night, and as they talked he pictured Martha's face. So animated, swept by light and shadow, grey eyes sparkling, soft brown hair falling around her shoulders.

"I met this strange old woman at the nursing home. She calls me Ronnie and keeps saying *vee gates.* You took German, didn't you? What does vee gates mean?"

Martha thought for a moment. *"Wie geht's.* That means — how's it going? You know. It's nearly the same in English!"

There were half a dozen parcels for Mrs Webster's the next day, and the day following. Gregory was beginning to feel quite at home now, mounting the front steps, pushing open the door, and greeting Ellen in the hall.

When Mrs Schwartz approached, he said "Vee gates?" cheerfully, and watched the old face crease in sheer delight.

"Iss gut!" said Mrs Schwartz. The small gold circles in her ears swayed gently with contentment.

It was such a little thing, thought Gregory, to please her so much.

By the end of the week the lower branches of the tree in Mrs Webster's hallway were brushing expectantly against the parcels piled at its foot.

Several of the ladies had taken to joining Mrs Schwartz, and Ellen showed each parcel all round, being careful to hold it specially close for Mrs Schwartz — "She can see red quite well, you know — bright colours!" she explained to Greg.

Mrs Schwartz had come to expect Gregory's jovial "Vee gates?" and her "Iss gut!" made his day.

ON Saturday he had a date with Martha, but his week's work began to tell on him, and he fell asleep during a film.

Afterwards they quarrelled, about his lack of interest, about his work — even about poor old Mrs Schwartz.

"If you were interested," Martha said crossly, "If you were the least bit interested in my company you wouldn't fall asleep when we were out together!"

"I didn't mean to," Gregory explained. "It was so hot, and I was tired —"

"I meant to ask you," said Gregory, "how would you say 'Merry Christmas' in German?"

"Fröhliche Weihnachten." Her voice was frigid.

"Well. I only asked."

"You interrupted me! It doesn't matter what *I* think. Your mind's on something else. Your job! That Mrs — what's-her-name, who calls you Ronnie. German even. Anything but me!"

One harsh word led directly to another, with Martha shouting and Gregory taunting back. Afterwards he wondered miserably just how it had begun.

He called her on Sunday, but she wasn't in. It was the same on Monday. Gregory felt depressed.

The bright spot in his day was Mrs Schwartz's face when he tried *"Fröhliche Weihnachten"* for the first time. Her old eyes, enormous behind the thick glasses, glowed with pleasure.

"Fröhliche Weihnachten!" she cried, as though she'd just remembered how. And Ellen clapped her hands and said to Gregory,

Continued on page 170

A versatile crocheted top, perfect for the beach or warm summer days. It could be worn with shorts, trousers or a pretty summer skirt.

Materials Required. — Of **Twilleys Springtime** 5 (6, 7, 7) x 50 gram balls; 3.50 mm and 4.00 mm crochet hooks.

For best results it is essential to use the recommended yarn. If you have difficulty in obtaining the yarn, write direct, enclosing a stamped, addressed envelope, to the following address for stockists: H. G. Twilley Ltd., Roman Mill, Stamford, Lincolnshire PE9 1BG.

Measurements. — To fit 81 (86, 91, 97) cm, *32 (34, 36, 38) inch,* bust; length, 45 (48, 51, 54) cm, *17¾ (19, 20, 21¼) inches.*

Tension. — 4½ groups and 6½ rows to 10 cm, *4 inches,* worked over pattern using 4.00 mm crochet hook.

Abbreviations. — Ch. — chain; h.tr. — half treble; d.c. — double crochet; s.s. — slip stitch; st(s) — stitch(es); sp. — space; tog. — together; ch.sp. — chain space; 2 tr. tog. — leaving last loop of each tr. on hook, work 2 tr. into next st. (or sp.), yarn round hook and draw through all 3 loops on hook; gr. — group — [2 tr. tog., 2 ch., 2 tr. tog.] all into same st. (or sp.); ins — inches; cm — centimetres.

N.B. Figures in brackets ( ) refer to the larger sizes; where only one figure is given, this refers to all sizes.

Back And Front (Alike).

With 3.50 mm hook make 65 (68, 71, 74) ch.

Foundation row. — 1 h.tr. into 3rd ch. from hook. 1 h.tr. into each ch. to end — 64 (67, 70, 73) h.tr.

Next row. — 2 ch., 1 h.tr. into each h.tr. to end.

Repeat last row 3 more times.

Change to 4.00 mm hook and work in pattern thus:

Next row. — 3 ch., miss 2 sts., *1 gr. into next st., miss 2 sts., repeat from *, ending with 1 tr. in turning ch. — 20 (21, 22, 23) grs.

It's The Tops!

Next row. — 3 ch., *1 gr. into 2 ch.sp., repeat from *, ending with 1 tr. in turning ch.

Repeat last row until work measures 30 (31, 32, 33) cm, *11¾ (12¼, 12½, 13) ins*, from beginning.

Shape Sleeves.

Next row. — 7 ch., 1 gr. into 5th ch., miss 2 ch., *1 gr. into next 2 ch.sp., repeat from * to end.

With a separate length of yarn make 5 ch., work over it thus: miss 1 ch., 1 gr. into next ch., miss 2 ch., 1 tr. in last ch. — 22 (23, 24, 25) grs.

Next row. — 3 ch., *1 gr. into 2 ch.sp., repeat from *, ending with 1 tr. in turning ch.

Continue straight in pattern until work measures 40 (41, 42, 43) cm, *15¾ (16¼, 16½, 17) ins.*

Shape Neck.

Next row. — 3 ch., *1 gr. into 2 ch.sp., repeat from * 7 (7, 8, 8) times more, 2 tr.tog. into next 2 ch.sp., turn.

Next row. — S.s. into 2 ch.sp. of 1st gr., 3 ch., 1 tr. into same ch.sp., *1 gr. into 2 ch.sp., repeat from * to end, 1 tr. into turning ch.

Next row. — 3 ch., *1 gr. into 2 ch.sp., repeat from * to end, 1 tr. into tr.

Next row. — 3 ch., *1 gr. into 2 ch.sp., repeat from * to end, 1 tr. in turning ch.

Repeat last row until work measures 45 (48, 51, 54) cm, *17¾ (19, 20, 21¼) ins.* Fasten off.

Miss 4 (5, 4, 5) grs., rejoin yarn to next 2 ch.sp. Complete to match first side, reversing shaping.

To Make Up.

Do not press. Join side and shoulder seams.

With 4.00 mm hook work 3 rows d.c. round neck and armholes. Work 1 row d.c. round hemline.

Continued from page 167

"You said it just like a native! My, that was absolutely wonderful!"

But on Tuesday everything went wrong again. There were twelve parcels on Tuesday. Twelve! He counted them, watched Ellen put them on the tree, prepared to leave, and then, wham! It came to him.

How had he missed a thing like that? How had he managed to come in every day, bring gifts, read names, and never realise?

He beckoned Ellen towards the door.

"Will there be something — what I mean is — isn't there anything for her?"

He indicated Mrs Schwartz, and Ellen shook her head.

"She hasn't anybody. Just that —" Her tone of voice made clear "that" was of no importance.

"But Mrs Webster won't see anyone left out! She gets something for everyone, so don't you worry!"

On Friday Martha phoned and they discussed (a) the weather, (b) how busy everybody was with only three more shopping days till Christmas, and (c) how silly they'd been last Saturday, and how on Christmas Eve there was this party one of Martha's arty friends was having, at which they would have a really good time.

It sounded wonderful! And afterwards there would be his very special present for Martha. He would give it to her and say . . . well he hadn't decided exactly *what* to say, but . . .

Why should he be worrying about Mrs Schwartz having nothing under the tree? It wasn't any of his business! It wasn't.

He had all his other presents bought, and when he got paid on Monday he'd have twenty-five pounds for Martha's, and he'd practically decided on the beautifully-bound art book because . . .

It was different for old people anyway. They'd had all their Christmases. They had no more need for wishing stars or bells that said ding-dong.

He'd buy the book on Monday.

And besides — she could get a parcel yet, couldn't she? There was still time.

But on Saturday, nothing came.

Ellen grinned, and pointed out the mistletoe she'd hung above the arch. She whispered, "There'll be cake and ice-cream on Christmas Eve, after they have opened up their presents."

"That's nice," said Gregory.

Although there was no delivery on Sunday, there was still Monday, wasn't there? and . . .

ON Monday morning he called round early. There was just one parcel for Mrs Clarke and another for Mrs Everly, but maybe someone else . . .

The tree was truly splendid now. Gifts underneath, around, beside, on top, with ribbons, bows, and tissue paper. It was a lovely sight.

He simply wouldn't ask. That way he wouldn't know for certain, and if he didn't know . . .

He looked at Ellen. Ellen shook her head. He swallowed angrily and seized the front door handle, turned it and slammed it behind him.

From the house next door, a radio blared out "Hark! the herald angels sing!" and Gregory thought, so let them! What could herald angels do? Who would make Christmas real for Mrs Schwartz?

He wished at once, of course, he hadn't asked that. Wished he'd never, never climbed the steps of Mrs Webster's nursing home or seen old Mrs Schwartz or said, *"Vee gates?"*

The truth, the sober, plain unwanted truth was, nobody cared but him.

He couldn't! Those art books were expensive. He needed twenty-five pounds. He really did!

What could he get Mrs Schwartz anyway? She couldn't see to read. Something to wear then?

The pottery was cheaper than the art books if —

But what? A scarf? Gloves? Never. She couldn't even go outside. There must be something.

He finished work at lunch-time. He had his lunch and . . . OK. He'd go to that shop in the city centre and get some little thing for Mrs Schwartz and get her out of his system.

IN the shop he walked through sweaters, nylons, nighties, slips, bras, panties, house-coats — and then he saw something. It was on a model with yellow hair and a plastic complexion: but it looked wonderfully warm and soft, and — it was red!

"How much is — that?"

"Twenty-two pounds, fifty."

The sales-lady fingered the soft dressing-gown and Gregory said, "Oh."

"It's reduced quite a bit actually. We haven't many dressing-gowns left, you know."

"It's — is there something — cheaper?"

"In what size?"

"That looks about right for size."

"What colour?"

"Red."

The sympathetic saleslady checked counters, drawers, the store rooms, but there was nothing in red.

"I'm sorry," said the saleslady. "I mean — that red one's all we have."

"It's perfect," Gregory said miserably.

"Do you want it gift-wrapped?" asked the saleslady.

There was barely time to buy a bottle of cologne with a silver

Continued on page 174

PERSONALITY PETS

THE FOX AT THE BOTTOM OF OUR GARDEN

BY MRS VERA LAKEY

ON holiday in Devon, we decided on a trip to the children's zoo. It was there that we saw a little fox in a cage. She was about three months old, the zoo-keeper said, and had been found abandoned in the woods nearby.

After that day, we made many more visits specially to see this little creature and grew quite fond of her. She had the appearance of a cuddly little puppy, but was very timid and shy.

We felt sad that this lovely little wild animal was doomed to a life confined in a small cage, never to roll on the grass or lie in the summer sunshine. So we decided to take her home with us.

The zoo-keeper agreed, but warned us the odds were very much against the little creature ever becoming domesticated. But, come what may, we just couldn't leave without her.

On arrival home we set to and built a large enclosure at the bottom of the garden, where our pet would be safe when not under supervision.

We had by this time decided to call her Sheba.

In the early stages Sheba was reasonably easy to manage but disliked to be touched or picked up. Coupled with her instinctive fear, she had probably been taught by her mother to mistrust man.

We knew that on hearing a human voice a vixen will snarl and growl to warn her cubs that danger is near. We also knew that Sheba would never forget her own mother's warning, and that she might never entirely trust us. However, that apart, she settled down quite nicely.

Sheba spent most of the day and evening in the house with the family and had a special corner of her own, where she curled up in a ball and watched all that went on with great interest.

Unfortunately she never learned to respect the house or its contents, and no amount of scolding made any difference.

For her own safety, we had to watch her every minute. Electric light flex, for instance, was irresistible to her. And all shoes ended up minus laces in no time — even when they were being worn!

So, with Sheba in the house, anything likely to get chewed had to be placed above floor level. Casual callers thought us rather a strange lot, with pairs of shoes on top of the piano and electric light flex draped around the picture-frames like Christmas chains!

We also had a problem with Tim our cat. We were never quite sure whether Sheba regarded him as a playmate or her next meal.

Tim, for his part, seemed quite puzzled by this strange creature who had invaded his kingdom. Sheba would shove him into a corner with her hindquarters and try to sit on him. Frantically, Tim would beat a hasty retreat — and join the shoes on top of the piano . . .

AT one-year-old, Sheba was fully-grown. Her behaviour in the house hadn't improved and we decided that perhaps the garden would be a more natural habitat.

It was too large to secure completely so we had to do the best we could and hope she would not want to escape.

It would have been unfair to pen her up after such freedom, so the choice was hers. We didn't want to lose her, and of course we worried that she would be unable to fend for herself after being in captivity for so long.

None of us slept well that night. Would she spend the dark hours frantically digging a hole under the fence?

Morning came at last, and I made a mad rush outside. What a mess! Our lovely garden was in a shambles. Reeds had been pulled out from the lily pond, the little plastic ducks were chewed to fragments, pots lay overturned, everything movable was in a different place.

But there, to everyone's relief, was Sheba, seemingly fast asleep in her pen. But, two very sleepy eyes peeped through her bushy tail, and we knew we need worry no more.

Although she looks much like a dog, her cleaning habits are that of a cat. She will lick herself clean, paws being used to wash face and behind ears.

She has a moult once a year in the springtime, when she will rub herself along the hedge to remove the thick, woolly coat that has kept her snug and warm throughout the winter.

She's dug a cosy den under the summer-house, a private place of her own, with three tunnels leading to it, instinct telling her this is the right thing for a fox to do. But she still needs a watchful eye. Anything missing from our home is almost sure to be found under the summer-house, tucked away for Sheba's future chewing sessions.

We have tried to give Sheba as normal a life as is possible. A London suburb garden can't be compared to the Devonshire countryside. But she seems content enough. We hope that she will be with us for many more years to come. Our garden would be a sad place without her. ■

Continued from page 171

ribbon for Martha before the shop closed. He got home as quickly as he could and dressed without spirit for the party.

"Of all the stupid things to do," he told his reflection grimly. Of all the — what would Martha think? A cheap bottle of cologne.

They had to be at the party early because Martha had to help with the sandwiches and decorations. He had his father's car, and he put both gifts in a bag on the back seat, Martha saw it at once and asked:

"What's in the bag?"

"Two parcels. I — if you don't mind — I've got one more delivery to make."

"Be as quick as you can, then, We've got an awful lot to do."

They raced across the bridge. The lights in Mrs Webster's evergreens had never shone so red, so green, so blue, and Martha breathed, "Oh, Gregory! It's beautiful!"

"I'll be right back," he said, and seized the bag.

He could hear the singing as he climbed the steps, and once inside, all Christmas broke upon him like a wave. The first presents were being opened, coloured paper was everywhere. Mrs Webster's Christmas tree glowed with self-satisfaction.

Ellen came to meet him, smiling a welcome.

"I — bought her something," Gregory said breathlessly.

"Please wait," said Ellen softly, "just while she opens it."

He was drawn in somehow, caught up, and time took on a Christmas Eve suspension. Around him was expectancy, and warmth and gratitude, and old, old faces staring at their memories.

"Iss beautiful!" said Mrs Schwartz. "Iss that you, *lieber* Ronnie?"

"That means 'dear' Ronnie," Ellen said. "Please stay and have some cake."

"Oh gosh! I can't —"

"Why not?" said Martha's voice from behind his shoulder. "There isn't any hurry. I mean, not really."

He stared. "How long . . ."

"I got cold in the car."

"Then you . . ."

"A gift like that," said Martha, "is expensive! It must have cleaned you out."

He nodded bleakly. "That's true."

"Stand here," said Martha. "Underneath the mistletoe."

She put both hands in his.

"Fröhliche Weihnachten, dear Gregory," she said softly. And she kissed him.

The old, tired faces around them beamed, and Ellen winked.

"Wie geht's?" she said.

"Iss gut!" Gregory sighed.

*** THE END ***